"*The Art of Kissing* goes beyond the valley of French kissing by exploring...such advanced exercises as the underwater kiss, the counterkiss and the electric kiss (rub your stockinged feet on the carpet and *whoa!*)."

—*Washington Times*

"Whoever said 'a kiss is just a kiss' didn't get his mitts on *The Art of Kissing*...a detailed how-to book...this year's handy alternative to chocolates."

—*Elle*

"Get it and expand *your* puckering portfolio."

—*Seventeen*

"It's refreshing to think about kissing per se rather than as a prelude to something else."

—*Self*

"If you...want to smooch like Rick and Elsa in *Casablanca,* this bussing bible is for you."

—Lowell (Massachusetts) *Sun*

"Some terrific tips on how you can make every kiss as passionate and thrilling as your first."

—*The National Enquirer*

"I advise you to race full speed to your bookstore and pick up a copy of *The Art of Kissing*...it could save you emotional problems."

The

Art of

Kissing

William Cane

ST. MARTIN'S PRESS
New York

For Carla Mayer Glasser

Production Editor: David Stanford Burr

Design by Susan Hood

Library of Congress Cataloging-in-Publication Data

Cane, William
      The art of kissing / William Cane.
          p. cm.
    ISBN 0-312-05378-9
     1. Kissing.   I. Title.
  GT2640.C36   1991
  394—dc20

                                   90-19117
                                     CIP

10 9 8 7 6 5 4

CONTENTS

PART THREE: KISSES FROM AROUND THE WORLD

PART FOUR: KISSING TECHNIQUE

$\mathcal{P}$REFACE

This book is the result of a kiss, and a rather embarrassing one at that. I had been kissing a certain young woman when she broke off and pushed away, her mouth a gaping oval of surprise and her blue eyes wide with shock and annoyance. I was taken aback by this sudden reversal of emotion: A moment before she had been kissing me passionately.

"You're not supposed to kiss with your eyes open," she said.

I was totally bewildered. Where in the book of kissing did it say that you had to kiss with your eyes closed? I asked her, but she couldn't tell me. "It's not nice to kiss and look," she insisted. And because she liked to kiss with her eyes closed I had to follow suit. That was her logic, and of course—being under her spell—I played by her rules.

But I was vexed, for I wanted to be able to refer to some authority to show that it was all right to kiss with your eyes open. Unfortunately the books on kissing that I consulted at the library were woefully silent on this and many other points. The best of the old books, *The Art of Kissing*, by Hugh Morris (1936), discussed a number of kisses in separate chapters, but its treatment was out-of-date and often consisted of merely a collection of quotes from classical poets. Neither Morris nor the other writers gave more than a perfunctory description of how to execute the kisses they discussed. It was as if they avoided detail on purpose.

Puzzled at the lack of explicitness in these works, I set out to obtain the information myself. Over a period of six years I gathered most of the data in this book through interviews and the first national survey devoted exclusively to the art of kissing. In all I surveyed more than three hundred people, collecting their responses to a comprehensive set of questions about every aspect of kissing.

In the process of writing the book I discovered that there is indeed an art to kissing. And although one can master the art without a book, it certainly helps to have a guide to what Ovid would call the weapons of the heart. Herein collected for your delight, amusement, and, O Pilgrim of Love, for your instruction, are the arts of Venus herself, the arrows I stole from the quiver of her little brat, all described in separate chapters, with dos and don'ts and helpful hints, and comments, too, from your friends and neighbors. Yes, your friends and neighbors, who would never tell you their deepest thoughts about kissing, those same men and women have told me all. And I'm going to let you in on their secret dreams and desires regarding kissing. Read the chapters in whatever order you like. Take notes, mark up the book, add your own ideas and impressions. If you're married or in a relationship, read it with your partner, or simply read it on your own and then surprise your lover with some unique kisses. Try one or two new ideas weekly. If you're not already in a relationship, all the better: You can study at your leisure, and you'll become an expert in no time.

Part One examines the psychology of kissing, dealing with emotional and sensual features and placing the subject in context. Part Two (The Kissing Encyclopedia) and Part Three (Kisses from Around the World) describe and explain in twenty-eight separate chapters how to execute familiar classics as well as the most exotic new kisses. Part Four examines almost every conceivable aspect of kissing technique, summarizing current practices, pinpointing what men and women like and don't like, and letting you benefit from the experiences of your contemporaries by covering such issues as whether you should keep your eyes open while kissing, how to kiss at parties, and when to kiss on a date.

Although in writing this book I relied upon the help and encouragement of people too numerous to list individually, I'd like to express my sincere appreciation to all who answered the kissing survey. Special thanks go to Susan Batkin for explaining at length what women like about kissing. I am indebted to Rhea Becker, Alison Galley, Debbi J. Karpowicz, and William McRell for listening to me read early drafts of the manuscript. For editing, and many excellent suggestions, I thank Barbara Anderson. For help with various stages of the publishing of the book, I thank Shirley Brownrigg, David Stanford Burr, Kate Dieterich, Marian Lizzi, and Jane Sherrill. Special thanks go to Carla Mayer Glasser for effort above and beyond that expected of an agent. And for their generous assistance, I thank my colleagues at Boston College, especially students from Techniques of Precise Expression. I am grateful to all those who gave invaluable suggestions, assistance, and encouragement, including: Ellen Abdow, Andrew Clark, Paul C. Doherty, Cathy Foley, Mark A. Fischer, Pierce Haley, Heather M. Kelley, Janelle Lawrence, Nina Murphy, Thomas J. Parello, Clara Silverstein, Cyndi Tracy, my parents, my sister, and my brothers. I could not have written the chapter on the Continental kiss without the expert opinion of Felix Pagliuca and Charles Bellone. Last but not least, thanks go to the librarians at the O'Neill Library at Boston College, the Mugar Library at Boston University, and the Boston Public Library.

THE ART OF KISSING

PART ONE

The
Psychology
of Kissing

WHAT IS KISSING?

Kissing appeals to almost everyone in Western culture, yet not many researchers have attempted to find out what it is that people like about the act itself. If the response to my kissing questionnaire is any indication, men and women everywhere are more than willing to voice their opinions. I even got replies from people who hadn't been sent the questionnaire. People almost gushed in their eagerness to talk about the subject, as if they had been deprived of an opportunity to share their innermost thoughts and feelings about this intimate form of lovemaking.

What do you like most about kissing?

WOMEN:

"I just love to kiss. It's the biggest turn-on."

"It lowers my blood pressure, warms my mood, and suppresses my appetite for sweet things, especially chocolate. I feel intoxicated (only with the right guy) and want to kiss for a long time. It's not necessarily a prelude to sex. It's a spiritual connection, exploring and devouring. Sometimes it makes me shake, sweat, laugh uncontrollably."

"It's a way of being close to someone but not necessarily intimate."

"Being able to vary it so much—French kiss, regular kiss, on the side of the mouth, biting, licking, sucking, exploring. It's never boring! And you have your hands free to touch other parts, too."

"Sexually, it's expressive . . . exciting . . . usually the first tactile contact you have with the other person. It's warming and brings you close. Nonsexually, it's affectionate, friendly."

"I like being physically close to the other person . . . the closeness, hugging, and arms intertwined, more than the actual kiss, except in unusual cases."

"The exploration, discovering the dance of it—the sensuality, give-and-take, slow arousal or immediate spark. The play—the way it can be a complete experience in itself and very erotic."

"How you can really express yourself with your kiss."

"The feeling of arousal that takes place! Someone who really knows how to kiss excites me totally. I love men who kiss into my ears—an erotic zone for me."

MEN:
"I like the oral nature of it. I'm an oral person. I drink, smoke, chew gum, bite my nails."

"The closeness of it. It's very sensuous. And you can do it anywhere, anytime. It's a quick way to show affection."

"Holding the other person—the physical touching."

"Feeling connected to my lover."

"It's where sex and romance meet. It's versatile, full of nuance. A kiss can tell. It communicates some important things about the people involved. This is true of a kiss on the lips. Anywhere else—less so."

Is there anything you don't like about kissing?

WOMEN:

"Smoker's breath!"

"I don't like to kiss anyone with bad breath or who slobbers (give kisses that are too wet)."

"Beard burn; bad breath; when it doesn't vary at all."

"Hard bruising kisses turn me off."

"If it's rough and painful it's awful."

"When a person isn't gentle or sensual: too deep and passionate a kiss before I'm ready for it. When a person glosses over kissing just to get to the next step."

"Being kissed with an open mouth when you only *like* the kisser."

"When people I don't know kiss me on the mouth. My brother-in-law kisses with his tongue out. Everybody hates to kiss him."

"Sometimes a man with no subtlety will thrust a pasty tongue into your mouth and it's like *oral rape*! A misfit of mouths. Or a man who has no passion in kissing. A too-delicate kisser can be irritating."

MEN:

"When her hair or fibers from articles of clothing get in the way."

"Having to pause to breathe. I've got an asthmatic problem, and mouth-breathing prohibits long kissing."

"When someone has bad breath (smoker's breath) or when someone dribbles."

"It's no fun when you have a cold."

Do you ever get very aroused simply by kissing?

WOMEN:

"Definitely! I feel light—like I'm walking in thin air. I love to kiss—it gets the body going."

"Absolutely. What's the point otherwise? (Okay, it's true, sometimes the intent of kissing is not sexual, but merely affectionate, apologetic, thankful, redemptive.)"

"Definitely! It makes my mouth tingle, my head gets dizzy, and my blood runs hotter through my veins."

"Yes, yes, yes, yes. I have a one-and-a-half-year friendship that includes only kissing and petting, and *boy* do I get aroused. It's amazing. Especially since I know it won't go further, it's also tantalizing."

"Arousal starts with the kiss for me. Okay, maybe it starts before that. But the kiss most definitely gets me moving along."

"Yes, if we're standing very close to each other."

"Yes. When kisses are very slow, gentle, wet, accompanied by light touches to the face and neck."

MEN:
"Positively yes."

"Ever? Always."

"Very. It's as close as you can get to anyone before it gets obscene in public. If you're Frenching, it's like giving yourself to one another."

"Yes. For example, a prolonged surprise kiss in the kitchen once led to kissing and cuddling on the living-room floor."

"Yes, but I think we were ready to be aroused, so kissing was the beginning."

"Yes, arousal occasionally leads to erection."

"The answer is yes."

What goes through your mind when you kiss?

WOMEN:
"Generally it's the physical sensations I'm aware of. Mentally I'm evaluating the kissing ability of the other person, the give-and-take and the response of the other person."

"How's he feeling? Does he really care for me? Does he like the *way* I kiss? What's going to happen if we both get out of control?"

"I like to see how turned on he gets. Usually it's as much as I do."

"It's about time he kissed me!"

MEN:

"I'm thinking about the kiss itself: 'Am I enjoying it? *What* am I enjoying about it? What am I going to do in return?' If I'm *not* enjoying it, *that's* what I'm thinking about."

"I don't believe my mind is active during a kiss."

"Warm, fond thoughts of the love I feel for my mate."

"I daydream about what she would be like if she were naked in bed. Sometimes I wonder what it would be like to be married to the person."

"One is to lose oneself in the moment. One is not thinking, but doing and being."

"What a lucky thrill I'm getting!"

"I often wonder what's next. Your mind immediately starts to think about sex and intercourse."

"A warm, relaxed feeling."

"How far I'll get with the girl."

Of course it's easiest to get some perspective on kissing by asking people about it directly, but for a truly comprehensive analysis we've got to make a brief detour into the realm of zoology. It's an incontrovertible fact that animals kiss, too. When anthropologist Jane Goodall studied chimpanzees at the Gombe National Park in Tanzania, Africa, she discovered that they kissed for a variety of different reasons and in a number of different social contexts. Some chimps kissed as a submissive gesture. They also kissed when greeting chimps they knew, or for what we would consider romantic reasons, such as when developing a relationship.

In her book *The Chimpanzees of Gombe* (Cambridge, Massachusetts: Harvard University Press, 1986) there is a wonderful picture of two chimps kissing in the jungle. The male's name is Humphrey, and he is sitting with his hands resting on the ground, his head tilted back, his mouth wide open, his eyes closed in pleasure. The female, Athena, is sitting in front of him, her right hand resting on top of his head with her thumb on his left eyebrow, her mouth also open as she kisses him. Goodall reports that the kiss lasted for more than thirty seconds, during which time both chimps panted.

Comparatively speaking, chimpanzee kisses are probably closest to human kisses, but many other species of animals also kiss, including horses during courtship, dogs during play, and even some fishes. Kissing fishes will often swim around with their lips locked to another fish's lips for hours in an exhibition of kissing stamina that few humans can match. Throughout the animal kingdom, then, kissing expresses tender emotions as well as strong sexual desire. But as for what's going through the mind of those fishes . . . your guess is as good as mine.

Next time you're with your lover, start a conversation about kissing animals. When you're trying to break the ice, describe a few kissing chimps or fishes for your partner, and I guarantee that it won't be long before the two of you are enjoying a few kisses of your own.

The

SENSUAL PLEASURE
OF KISSING

"I enjoy kissing more than intercourse sometimes," a thirty-six-year-old woman said. "There's nothing like two people exploring each other's mouths on the same wavelength."

"Kissing is a gesture of affection and I like the spontaneity of it," said another young woman. "It's nice for a kiss to be separate sometimes from a sexual experience; lots of people don't understand this."

"Many men think kisses always should lead to intercourse, so I usually don't get *too* involved with kissing unless I want to end up making love."

"Kissing by itself can be very sensual and sexy and is not just part of a ritual before sex."

"Kissing is great. It's very important, not just as an opening for sex."

"It's my favorite thing to do (sexually)."

"Kissing is wonderful fun if taken lightly and a prelude to rich intimate relations if taken seriously. I like to be clear with whomever I'm kissing which it is going to be."

"America needs more kissing; maybe the divorce rate wouldn't be so high."

"We need more kissing, less fighting; more hugging, too."

The opinions of these young women represent a bold new way of looking at the sensual aspects of kissing. They're suggesting that kissing often can and should stand alone as a sensual pleasure that deserves to be enjoyed for itself without going on to other sex acts. Kissing can bring two people closer than ******** because it's a more personal interaction. Which is why many prostitutes won't kiss their customers. They'll ******** for hours but won't kiss because kissing is considered even more intimate than ********!

The past few years have witnessed a ground swell of new interest in kissing as a contemporary generation of lovers redefines what it considers romantic. Recent sex surveys indicate that modern lovers believe kissing is one of the most essential aspects of a relationship, yet men and women are increasingly reporting that there is not enough kissing in their love lives. For example, a recent survey of more than 4,000 men showed that of all foreplay activities kissing was considered the most enjoyable. At the same time another survey—*The Hite Report on Male Sexuality*—indicated that many men want more kissing in their relationships. And *The Hite Report* itself, just like the women quoted at the start of this chapter, revealed that many women rated the pleasure they received from kissing higher than the pleasure they received from any other type of sexual activity, yet they frequently complained that there wasn't enough kissing in their love lives. Lovers take note: There is a growing interest on the part of women and men in the nongenital aspects of sexual intimacy, including kissing, all of which suggests that kissing is perhaps the most sensuous form of loveplay. Indeed, a lot of people like it so much that they seem to think that they are somehow alone in their insatiable desire to kiss. Many people told me confidently: "I like to kiss more than just about anybody!"

Let's admit that we like to kiss and move on to something more arcane and at the same time more practical.

Kissing is a normal human activity, but there is more to it than you may at first suspect. Believe me, there's more to it than I ever suspected when I sent out the first batch of questionnaires. Every time I received a reply in the mail I felt an unaccountable thrill of expectation and anticipation and was rarely disappointed.

The following chapters chronicle the secret, strange, and utterly wonderful kissing techniques of hundreds of people who anonymously voiced their private thoughts and feelings about every aspect of contemporary kissing practices. Consult the kissing encyclopedia and the kisses from around the world section to brush up on such standards as French, lip, or neck kisses. Use those chapters to perfect the fine points of kisses you've tried only once or twice; and let them inspire you to venture into the realm of new kisses you may never have heard of before, kisses so exotic and wild that you'll hesitate to try them with any but your most intimate partner.

PART TWO

The

Kissing

Encyclopedia

The

$\mathscr{F}$IRST KISS

Not surprisingly, most people can remember their first kiss; whether it happened ten or fifty years ago, it seemed to have left an indelible impression on them.

Do you remember your first kiss?

Can remember	90%
Can't remember	6%
No response	4%

What was your first kiss like? Who did you kiss? Did you enjoy it? How did you feel the next day?

WOMEN:

"My first kiss with G– was in my room. I was seventeen years old. We were listening to music, and the moment was right. We leaned toward each other, and I knew we were about to kiss. In anticipation I shut my eyes and puckered up, ready for my lips to meet his. They never did . . . he had his mouth *open* instead of puckered, so instead of meeting his lips, I met his tonsils! When I suddenly felt this big wet mouth encompassing my face (no joke, he got my nose, my chin . . .), I burst into hysterical laughter. My first kiss with G– started out so romantically, and ended up with me curled up on the floor giggling!''

"I was a sixteen-year-old virgin. I was on a visit to Ireland and was in a nightclub. All at once a stranger grabbed and kissed me. I enjoyed it. I'd never been kissed, so I felt very flattered; a little confused, because he disappeared back into the crowd. I would have liked to have found out more about him. Next day I felt as if I'd reached an important milestone. But I did want to know more about kissing; I had a very strict upbringing so it was impossible for me to experiment with kissing. I imagined kissing a man, using my thumb and forefinger as a mouth. My family were not affectionate or *kissy*. I wanted more kissing experiences. That stranger sparked my interest."

"My heart exploded. I was one happy rubber-chested gal the next day. A New Year's party. I was fourteen or fifteen. His name was Gary, a boy my age, a schoolmate. My first experience drinking hard liquor (or any kind of liquor). I let him touch my breasts under my shirt. We kissed for hours on a couch in a den of a friend's house. Then he drove me to a place where we watched planes take off from the airport, soaring, blasting close overhead. More kissing. More thrill to the bone marrow. I still remember his breath, and occasionally the scent comes back to me."

"I felt very excited and couldn't wait to be kissed again. I was approximately ten and kissed the boy across the street."

"I was sixteen. I kissed a boy I had known for a while. I

enjoyed it. It happened near the end of the summer as four of us were driving home from a dance in *his* car. He got the other boy to drive so we could sit in back. He leaned forward to tell him something about the car and kissed me as he turned around toward me. I definitely got turned on. I had been afraid I wouldn't be kissed by sweet sixteen.''

"It was heady, exhilarating, and oh, so cool. I was thirteen, he was fourteen—our fathers were old friends. We were playing 'Murder in the Dark' in my cousin's parents' bedroom in Karachi, Pakistan. The adults were outdoors, the kids inside. He and I flirted a bit, just joking around in a teasing way. Clearly not kids but teenagers. His name was Jani and he was androgynous (not a stud), playful, and, most important, attentive to me! I think that when the lights first went off, he touched me. And I thrilled to his touch. The next time the lights went off, he came toward me, knowing where I was sitting (I stayed put), and just grabbed me and kissed me. It felt . . . magnificent . . . *beautiful*. Electrified. Energized. Sexy! We played 'Murder in the Dark' a few more times that summer. What a summer! 1977.''

"I was twelve. He was a fourteen-year-old guy who was in a play with me in junior high. We had the two lead parts, and we fell in love. It was opening night of the play and we were waiting backstage. The play was a Western and I was a saloon girl, so I had bright lipstick on. One of the guys who used to flirt with me said, 'Madam, let me take that lipstick off your face,' then attempted to kiss me. Instead, Tom (my boyfriend-to-be) stepped in and said, 'No, let me do it.' He took me in his arms, leaned me back Hollywood style, and gave me a long, slow French kiss. I was thrilled and excited. The play went great! The next day I felt more mature and definitely happy.''

"I was thirteen when I kissed my first boyfriend, Peter. Yes, I enjoyed it. It almost felt like we were doing something that we weren't supposed to. It was so soft and gentle. It was great."

"I was seventeen and had a year-long crush on a neighborhood gas station attendant. He was twenty-five or so and knew of my crush. He was leaving the state, and on his last day at work I secretly planned to meet with him. I met him after work, and after driving around a bit, we parked. (In the year that I had known him, we had never kissed or verbally expressed our feelings about each other.) We sat making small talk. The car had bucket seats, and I was quite nervous and wasn't looking at him. He gently took my hand, which was resting on the console. My heart started beating fast. I wanted to kiss him but didn't want to make the first move. Slowly, we leaned toward each other. The initial kiss happened almost in slow motion as our lips finally met. What was so special about it was the buildup (waiting for the year), his gentleness (he wasn't aggressive or pushy), the secrecy, our genuine attraction. When I think of the kiss itself I think of all these things. The kiss felt natural and carried with it the energy of what I'd expected a first kiss to have."

MEN:
"I was fourteen years old, and I kissed a girl I had a crush on named Karen. It felt great, though she was eight inches taller than I was. I felt like I was floating on a cloud. I was a little embarrassed because she kissed me in front of my whole soccer team."

"I was in fourth grade and played Spin the Bottle. I was mostly surprised with how soft and slippery her lips were."

"I was about ten. Who did I kiss? It was possibly Karen M–, unfortunately not Loretta F–. We played Postman and Spin the Bottle at birthday parties in the fifth and sixth grades. I really loved it; have ever since. I knew from the start that I was blessed at it, too."

"We were both in ninth grade and she was my high school sweetheart. I enjoyed it but thought it was too slurpy, too moist."

"I was seventeen, and she was eighteen and the most beautiful girl at college—straight fairish hair, blue eyes that always seemed to be smiling wistfully at you, a body like Brigitte Bardot's—and she was the nicest person, so affable, outgoing, and friendly that I often thought of her as a sister. We were just friends, but there was an undercurrent of sexual attraction between us. The party was at her house, and when I was leaving she walked with me to the door and stood talking to me for a minute. I suddenly became bold and asked if I could kiss her. She thought about it for a moment, and I was getting set for her to say no, when she smiled and said all right. I couldn't believe it! I felt electricity shooting through my nerves; she was such a receptive kisser that our souls seemed to melt into each other. I'll never forget that kiss."

How to overcome shyness

Some people like to savor the shyness of the first kiss. It gives them an all-choked-up-inside feeling, and for them the initial shyness is what makes the first kiss so memorable. But excessive shyness can hinder your enjoyment. Here's how to reduce your first-kiss jitters:

1. Arrange to have that first kiss in a fun or playful context. One woman used this technique successfully by telling her boyfriend (who had come over to help paint the living room) that she wanted to go steady with him. When he readily agreed, she quickly said they should seal it with a kiss—and before he could say anything she leaned forward and kissed him. That first kiss lasted no more than a fraction of a second, but it did a lot to break the ice. Kissing under mistletoe is another example of using a nonthreatening situation to get things started.

2. Get close enough to the other person so that your feelings take control. The key is to get within kissing distance, which is about one foot away from him—so close that you can feel his body heat. This is why lovers often make believe they see something in their partner's eye. One woman reports that she steps up to her boyfriend and asks him what he thinks of her perfume. Anything to get him close will usually do the trick. If you're both ready for the kiss and you get close enough, it happens automatically.

3. Simply ask for the kiss. Sometimes it's even appropriate to make a demand: Remember Shakespeare's line from *The Taming of the Shrew*: "Kiss me, Kate!" You can start the ball rolling with the same line. Said one young woman: "One time I told a boy I was dating that if he didn't kiss me soon—we would *stop* dating."

4. For a more subtle approach, catch your partner's eye when you're out together. Most men say they take their cue about kissing from the woman, usually from observing her behavior toward them. If she stands close, smiles warmly, holds eye contact, and generally looks like she wants to be kissed, then the man feels encouraged to initiate the kiss. You can often tell if a man wants to kiss

you by looking at his eyes; if he's staring at your mouth he's ready to kiss you. After you've gone on a few dates, watch him closely when you're saying good night. When you see him staring at your mouth, stop whatever you're doing and look dreamily at him, and usually he'll take the hint and kiss you.

What advice can you give to a shy person?

"Relax and enjoy. There's no correct way to kiss, so don't worry about doing anything wrong."

"Just do it. It's trial and error."

"Let loose and don't worry about what you look like up close; usually the other person's eyes are closed."

"Go for it!"

"Take it slow and gently and learn your partner's response and react by reciprocating."

"Don't do it unless you're ready."

"Start slow and gradually let yourself go; loosen up."

"Go slowly, softly, and with great attention."

"Don't be shy; it's the greatest thing."

"Just pucker up and plant one on your partner's lips."

"Don't think about it; just let it happen."

"Relax and don't be uptight—it'll happen. If you think too much you might just screw it up."

"Let the other person take the initiative. Don't look too pushy."

"Don't suffocate your partner and don't shun his or her tongue."

"Be yourself, be confident, express your feelings."

How to make all your kisses feel like first kisses

The secret of erotic kissing is to make each and every kiss feel like a first. Here's how to recapture the thrill that usually accompanies a first kiss:

1. Think of your lover as a stranger. According to many anthropological studies, the stranger—the person from another clan or tribe—is invested by the primitive mind with extraordinary sexual energy. It is not clear why this is so, but the principle suggests a very effective way to make your kisses come alive. Try to imagine that you're meeting your lover for the first time. Many men and women mentioned that they used this technique successfully in their loveplay.
2. It sometimes helps to go to new places, new settings, because this acts as a spur to the imagination.
3. Become fascinated with some delightful aspect of your lover and focus on this so that you become almost hung up on it. If you can become obsessed with some aspect of your lover—his arms, or the delicate flecks of light in his eyes, or the curve of the neck—you will magnify that aspect out of all proportion and the person will appear

new to you. The key is to become involved with the here and now.

4. Don't anticipate. Sometimes lovers get into a rut, anticipating what will happen next, looking forward to the usual patterns that their lovemaking takes. In order to break out of this rut, tell yourself that you're *not* going to go on in your usual way, that you're simply going to dally and play for a while. Then settle down to some dallying and playing. Take your time.

5. Observe cats. Method actors like Marlon Brando studied them to learn how to concentrate. Observe how the cat looks at something. All the animal's attention is devoted to what it is watching. Do you look at your lover in the same way? Do you dote on your lover? Learn to look at your lover the way a cat looks at a ball of string—with total and undivided concentration.

The first kiss can be attempted and successfully executed in a number of ways. The most popular way is to get to know the person and then get physically close. For those who have been kissing for years and who thought it was all downhill from here—it isn't! By following some of the suggestions given above, you can experience the wonder of the first kiss all over again. Stage actors face this challenge each time they have to play a scene before a new audience. Alas, your audience may not always be new, but your kissing can be if you concentrate on the experience.

The

ℒIP KISS

"Sometimes when I look at a stranger's lips close up and they look quite kissable, I think, 'Oh, I would like to kiss those lips!' " In saying so, didn't this twenty-five-year-old woman voice a feeling common to all lovers? In fact, both men and women have told me that they regularly daydream about lips. A moist red bow parted over a set of even white teeth . . . Ah, it's a natural invitation to kiss! Which is why some people will even kiss a picture in a magazine. And which is why all lovers should keep their lips kissable: If your lips are cute and moist they'll draw others toward you with irresistible allure.

Sure, the lip kiss is the most basic kiss, and you do it by simply puckering up, moving close, and pressing your lips to your lover's. But such a description is only the beginning of the story. Said one young woman: "I enjoy the *creativity* behind kissing—the many combinations possible using the lips." *The many combinations!* This is the key. And yet all you really need to know to get started is how to approach, what to do during the kiss, and how to break off.

How to approach

Imagine that your lover's lips are pressed together in a demure red bow. Try simply touching your closed lips to the lips of your lover. What passion such a simple initial encounter can generate! You hold back and remain lethargic, not opening your lips the slightest, simply touching them lightly to your lover's. That simple contact will be enough to excite you both to the core, and you'll feel the blood beating in each other's lips.

Another approach is to move in carefully so that you make contact with only your lover's lower lip. As soon as you make contact, stop and simply settle into the kiss slowly and softly, savoring the warmth of your lover's flesh.

Initial lip contact can also be made rather haphazardly, slowly, almost hypnotically as the result of prolonged eye contact. After you've been talking with a lover for a long time, if you've been sitting close and looking into each other's eyes, you'll feel a tension mounting between you that almost draws the two of you together. Let this tension build, and as your faces get close don't worry if your noses bump; simply tilt your head slightly and press onward until your lips touch.

What to do during the kiss

Unfortunately even in this revolutionary age some people are still skittish about kissing. Once they make lip contact they seem to be in a rush to break off. They may unconsciously think that lip contact is dirty or nasty or prohibited, and these ideas may make them afraid of longer kisses. Such myths interfere with real enjoyment. You've got to learn to settle down, relax, and enjoy the lip kiss. "During a kiss I think about the feel of my partner's lips," said one woman. "I think about the positions of our bodies." Move your limbs into various comfortable positions. Keep in mind that horses will stand together necking for hours, and try to achieve this same animal delight in closeness. Here are some specific tips on what to do during the lip kiss:

- Move your lips slightly back and forth.
- Be active and press your lips forward.
- Suck your partner's upper or lower lip.
- Sway your head back and forth gently.
- Become passive and let your partner lead.

How to break off

There comes a point during every kiss when you've had enough. Some people fear that they might insult their partner by breaking off, and as a result they let a worn-out kiss go on forever. If you're enjoying a really long kiss, all well and good. But when the time comes, you've got to know how to break off. Don't just rip your mouth away unless you want to alarm your lover. Slowly close your lips while they're still in contact with your partner, and pause. Notice whether your partner is initiating another kiss. If your partner is starting another kiss, then you must decide whether you still want to break off. If so, keep your lips closed and pull back gently. At that point open your eyes, and you're where you can either kiss again or withdraw further or receive another kiss from your lover.

Other techniques for ending a kiss include:

- Stop any lip movement and become passive. Then simply wait for your lover to end the kiss.
- Pull back quickly. This method of ending may startle your lover, but it can be a funny way to end a kiss now and then, and can often lead into a teasing kiss where your partner will lean forward in order to continue the kiss, with you leaning farther back to tease.
- Make a little *mnnh*! sound and gently lean back until you break lip contact.

The

$\mathcal{E}$YE KISS

You're kissing your boyfriend, let's say, when you happen to open your eyes and notice that he's got a very sweet expression on his face. He's also got his eyes closed. You've been kissing his lips, but the way he looks with his lashes demurely down gives you ideas so that you begin to kiss him on his cheek at the side of the mouth, and then little by little, giving him a series of rather quick kisses as you go, you begin to travel up the side of his face to his eyes, where you softly place the lightest, most tender kisses you can deliver, first on one eye and then on the other.

For such an unusual kiss, a surprising 40 percent of women and 60 percent of men said they liked it. Because the eye kiss has tender and romantic connotations, it occasionally appears in love stories. In chapter six of Hemingway's *A Farewell to Arms*, Frederic kisses his lover with some eye kisses. First he gives her a regular kiss, almost to pave the way for the eye kiss. Then when he sees that her eyes are shut, he kisses both her shut eyes.

Tips for kissing the eyes

- Start with other kisses to lull your partner into a relaxed and receptive state.
- When your partner closes his or her eyes, kiss one shut eye gently, then the other.
- Return often to the lips to keep your partner satisfied. Think of eye kisses as a novelty, a diversion.
- After a few soft eye kisses, you can lick the eyelids or kiss the eyes more forcefully.
- If your partner is wearing contacts be extra careful.

The

ℰAR KISS

So few people kiss the ears! But if the ears could speak, they'd tell us, no doubt, that as with nose, eye, and neck kisses, the ear kiss is special because it's a one-way kiss: Your lover can't kiss you back until after your kiss is completed. As a result the burden is upon you to make the kiss sensual and satisfying. But with the ear kiss you're helped by the fact that the sounds of your breathing and the other little sounds that occur during the kiss will stimulate your partner. Exploit all these aspects of the kiss and your lover will surely thrill to the sound and feel of your ear kisses.

Tips for ear kisses

- Kiss the ear as if it were a mouth. *Smack, smack, smmmmmmack!*
- Kiss the earlobe as if it were a lower lip: suck it and nibble on it, occasionally tugging on it with your lips and teeth.
- Gently insert your tongue into the ear. Trace the ridges and hollows with a light touch.
- Clamp your mouth over the entire ear, trying to swallow it whole.

- Make little *mmmmmmmmmmmmm* and *uhhhhhhhh* sounds. Heartfelt *oohs* and *aahs* are also a turn-on at this time.
- Breathe softly into your partner's ear. The sound of your breathing will be exciting. The tickle of your lips and of your warm breath will be a unique delight.
- Whisper things to your partner. Appropriate comments include such phrases as, "I love you," "You're so sweet," and "Oh, darling." A really nice thing to say at this moment is, "I love your ears."

10 percent of men, and 85 percent of women like ear kisses.

MEN:

"I like having my earlobes tugged at by my lover's teeth."

"I sometimes laugh when she kisses my ears, but it's a laugh of intense pleasure."

WOMEN:

"I like to be kissed on the ears occasionally, depending on who it is."

"It drives me crazy."

"For ear kisses the timing must be right. I need a lot of mouth kissing first."

"I enjoy the slurping and breathing sounds when I'm being kissed on and in my ear."

"Not the ears. I hate that."

"Yes, but only if it's in the frame of foreplay. I hate it in public."

"I especially like being kissed on my neck and ears."

The

𝒩OSE KISS

Imagine that you're a young man kissing your girlfriend one morning when she suddenly starts kissing your nose. Would you react like a friend of mine did?

"Don't kiss my nose," he said.

"Why not?" his girlfriend asked. "You have a nice nose and I like kissing it."

"Kissing the nose is kind of . . . infantile."

But she continued kissing his nose, and the fellow had to suffer it in silence. He later admitted that he did enjoy it, though he felt surprised at first because it was so unusual.

The nose is one of the erogenous zones that Freud overlooked in his analysis of human sexuality, but it's an organ that deserves to be revitalized in sexual stature. Indeed, survey results show that 40 percent of women and 55 percent of men like being kissed on the nose.

A nose kiss is easy to do; simply put your lips to your lover's nose and kiss away . . . all along the length of it, right up to the spot between the eyes, and then down again to the nostrils. And if the nostrils are cute you kiss them, too, licking, even inserting your tongue, and playing around.

While you're at it, remember that you've left your partner's lips idle. You don't want to spend *too* much time dallying with the nose since lip kisses are infinitely more satisfying. Return unfailingly to the lips, but come back now and then to the nose kiss as a brief little respite from a series of lip kisses.

The first few times you kiss your partner's nose, be prepared for complaints. Although *your* mouth is occupied, your partner's is free, so get ready for protests, jokes, and sarcasm. Usually he'll complain about what you're doing, how unusual it is, and so on. My advice? If he has a nice nose, kiss it and let him babble on all he wants.

The

ℛECK KISS

The most surprising thing that the kissing survey revealed was that (aside from the mouth) of all the places that women like to be kissed, their favorite spot was the *neck*. More than 94 percent of women rated it as a highly erotic zone. And while three out of four men also liked to be kissed on the neck, none of them came close to raving about it the way women did. Conclusion? Kiss her neck! And, gals, if he doesn't know by now, tell him. Imagine some poor fellow going through his entire marriage not knowing that his wife is driven wild by neck kisses. This chapter is for him. All the quotes are by women, who were much more eloquent on this kiss than men.

"I was fifteen when I had my first intense kissing encounter. I was sitting in the den with my boyfriend, and I was getting very excited while he was kissing my neck. It was the first time I had had my neck kissed in this way. I was moaning quite loudly and getting very turned on, and my boyfriend asked, 'Are you all right?' I felt I had to explain why I was so excited. Not having had much experience in kissing, I was embarrassed. Was *I* overdoing it? Just how excited should I have been? In retrospect I wouldn't have reacted as I did."

"To have a man come up behind me, breathe on my neck, and bite me, kiss me there is to send a thousand volts through my spine."

"I like to be kissed on the eyes, nose, ears, neck, shoulders, and arms—everywhere! The neck drives me crazy."

"Kissing, licking, or biting my neck is an incredible turn-on."

"Of the eyes, nose, shoulders, and arms, I especially like neck kisses."

"Ears and neck are my favorite spots."

"I go crazy when someone kisses my neck. *That* is very sexually arousing to me."

"Drives me nuts!"

"Drives me crazy!"

How to kiss the neck

1. After a few lip kisses, drop down and kiss the side of the neck. This move ensures a smooth transition from lip to neck kisses.
2. Place tender kisses in the hollow of the neck, which is that small cuplike depression that the chin touches when you bend your head all the way forward. Then lick that little cup as if you were drinking from it. If your lover is lying down, you can actually fill the hollow with grape

juice and lap it up, doggy style. This is guaranteed to drive your lover crazy.

3. Exhale your warm breath onto the back of your lover's neck as if to mark it for a kiss. Then bite and kiss the spot.

4. Strange as it may sound, you can study pictures of Dracula to get more pointers on technique. For example, in the film *Taste the Blood of Dracula*, Dracula (Christopher Lee) faces the woman and with both hands on her shoulders leans down and bites the side of her neck. In another scene he stands behind her, his right hand on her right shoulder, his left hand pinching the left side of her neck, while he prepares to bite the right side of her neck. The same positions can be used for tender kisses or playful love nips.

The

8LECTRIC KISS

Everyone has experienced small shocks from static electricity. When you take off a sweater or walk across a carpet, you built up an electrical potential in your body that is neutralized when you touch something or someone. These facts form the principle behind the electric kiss. The kiss is perfectly safe, but if you follow these suggestions it's sure to give you and your lover a charge.

How to get ready for the electric kiss

First shut off the lights. You'll see why in a moment. Now rub your feet back and forth on the rug. It's not necessary for your lover to do the same; one charged party will suffice for this kiss. When you rub your feet on a rug, you build up an excess of negative electric particles and become negatively charged, primed for a small electrical shock when you touch something or someone who is positively charged or uncharged—that is, electrically neutral.

Now slowly approach the other person. Let's assume the

negatively charged person is a woman. Step up to the man and, without touching him with your legs or hands, bring your face close to his. You must be careful not to touch him with any part of your body, because if you do you'll neutralize the electrical field and the sparks won't fly when you kiss him.

At this point your lips are getting closer to his and in the dark you can barely see his face. You have to be careful. Listen for the sound of his breathing and use that like an airplane pilot uses a homing signal to guide the plane into the airport. Home in on his breathing. At this crucial and romantic moment, you may want to whisper a few amorous words to him, such as:

"Hold steady now. Don't move."

This will ensure that he is in position for your kiss. Move in slowly, ever so slowly. Part of the fun of this kiss is getting close and intimate without touching. Can you do it? It takes a bit of will power and even a bit of practice.

As your lips close within a fraction of an inch, a tiny electric spark will jump across from your lips to his. If you're looking down at this precise moment, you'll see a scintillating flash of light, like fireworks. This is the electricity that poets and novelists have written about for years. And now for the first time you and yours have made it all visible. Sparks of love! The excitement of the moment is usually enough to cause some young lovers to jump back in surprise. But you are a hardy soul and forge ahead. If you have been listening intently, you will have even heard the tiny crack and pop of the electricity as it jumps from your puckered lips to his. Now is the time to lean forward and kiss him. For right now your lips are tingling with a spent electrical charge, and there is no better relief from the tiny electric shock than the sweet sensation of a soft kiss. Ah!

The most famous electric kiss in English literature appears at the end of Henry James's *The Portrait of a Lady:* "His kiss was like white lightning, a flash that spread, and spread again, and stayed." Indeed the physical forces at work in the electric kiss are the exact same physical forces that cause thunderstorms and lightning.

It's fun to use the electric kiss to surprise someone who doesn't know anything about it. For example, if your lover is wearing a sweater, ask him to take it off. The simple act of removing a sweater, especially a woolly one, is usually enough to give him a powerful electrostatic charge. You may have to caution him to keep his hands behind his back and close his eyes. Tell him you have a surprise for him. Some men get so excited at such a suggestion that they don't even feel the shock of the kiss because their entire body is filled with energy and anticipation. If this happens, you know you need to sensitize him. Explain the kiss to him. If he's patient enough to listen to a description of a unique new kiss—and it takes a certain lighthearted sense of play to appreciate this one—you know you've found a good lover. Anyone willing to go through the preparatory steps of shutting off the lights, getting charged up, being careful enough not to touch you, and moving extremely slowly into the kiss is someone you'll enjoy kissing with high-voltage electric kisses.

Where to do electric kisses

One young woman told us that she tried the electric kiss on her boyfriend after a party when they were standing in the hallway to go home. The air was dry and there was a big shag rug on the floor. The conditions were perfect. The shock was so strong that the fellow jumped back and wanted to know whether she was hooked to an electrical gag. He thought she was crazy for a while, and he was afraid to approach her until she explained what she was doing. Then he couldn't get enough of it. They stayed there for twenty minutes shocking each other with what seemed like lightning bolts from their lips. She reported that his mouth felt so tender and sweet after the shocks that she was tingling for hours afterward. This illustration suggests that the setting for the electric kiss must be just right. If you pick the setting carefully, your experience will not only be shocking but also highly romantic.

The electric kiss will work in the following locations, each of which has been rated by a master electrician in volts. (Ratings from 55 to 1,000 volts will give you a nice, harmless shock, not enough to hurt you by any means. Ratings over 1,000 volts can be slightly painful.)

On a couch	55 volts
In a movie theater	66 volts
On a shaggy rug	625 volts
In a hotel lobby	800 volts
In a department store	75 to 1,000 volts
Under a wool blanket	250 to 4,000 volts

The

$\mathcal{B}$ITING KISS

Consider the typical businessman. He wears a gray suit and a gold watch. He carries a briefcase inside of which are papers he'll work on during the taxi ride to the office. He's usually able to concentrate on his work, but on this particular trip into the center of the city his mind wanders. Through the taxi window he sees people walking to work. He spots a good-looking woman in a blue dress, and suddenly he's thinking back to the night before when Luella was biting his earlobes.

"What's so funny?" the cabbie says, looking at him in the mirror.

"Oh, nothing," he says. "I was just thinking of something."

The biting kiss is the kind of kiss they remember the next day. So don't shy away from using your teeth; 70 percent of men and 62 percent of women said they like to be bitten (gently!) by their lover when things get passionate. Said one man, "A little nipping kiss turns me on and tells me she's turned on, too."

The biting kiss is at once sophisticated and sensual, playful and serious. It's a kiss of affection, of deep desire, of controlled aggression. Every lover should master it fully; whether or not you like to do it, you should know how it's done, just in case the urge comes upon you to bite—or be bitten.

How to deliver a biting kiss

1. Gently nip your lover's flesh between your front teeth.
2. Tug up a fraction of an inch.
3. Release the flesh and let it slip back through your teeth.
4. As you release the flesh, move immediately in toward the skin again and nip the flesh between your teeth once more.
5. Repeat the first four steps as you move slowly over the neck, arms, and face.
6. You can vary the kiss by nipping the flesh between your lips only, so that your teeth don't directly touch your lover's flesh.

Dos and don'ts of the biting kiss

Do:

- Be gentle.
- Nip deep enough into the flesh so that you can actually tug at it with your teeth. If you're careful it won't hurt. Prolonged execution of this kiss can scratch, however, making the skin sore. Use your judgment as to when enough is enough.
- Ask your partner whether he or she likes it.
- Break up the biting kiss with other types of kisses. For example, after you've done a few biting kisses on your lover's arm, you should kiss it with gentle little kisses.

- Do be aware of your inner reactions. The biting kiss can arouse subtle aggressive feelings within you. Psychologists and poets have told us that love involves some element of aggression, and the biting kiss will let you get in contact with it in the most playful way. At the same time, recipients of the kiss can get in contact with their feelings of submissiveness and subservience. These feelings are part of the normal give-and-take of any love relationship and can be experienced during the biting kiss in a safe context.

DON'T:

- Don't try it on a first date. Know your lover before you venture into the realm of the biting kiss.
- Don't draw blood, or don't draw an excessive amount.
- Don't hurt your partner.
- Don't try the biting kiss through clothes, only on bare flesh. If you try it through clothes you'll just get your mouth full of lint.

Do you like to bite or be bitten when kissing?

WOMEN:

"A little nip may be tolerable, but that's all."

"I like to be bitten gently on my neck."

"Yes, especially on my neck and ears. Wow!"

"Yes, yes, yes, both. I admit I do like to bite a little. Not so much on the mouth but certainly on the neck."

"I like biting and being bitten when kissing, but it's got to be gentle."

"I love it."

"Yeah. Just so that you feel your teeth. Just a little. You don't have to break skin."

"My partner bites all over, including my tongue and lips. But I'm not too excited about it."

"I love my lower lip to be bitten when being kissed. I could playfully bite my partner for hours."

"Yes, if kissing other parts of the body besides the lips."

"A nibble or a tug here and there is nice. I like having my earlobes tugged at, or little half-bites around the collar. I pull on my own lip once in a while (with my teeth) to kiss with only the lower or upper lip—which is more of a bump than a kiss."

If you're reluctant to try the biting kiss, consider only one thing. Have you ever seen two puppies rolling around on the floor biting and nipping playfully at each other? When you bite your lover you regress to a primitive level and sex becomes freer and more liberating. Engaging in a little aggressive loveplay, teasing each other now and then with nipping biting kisses, can get rid of a lot of inhibitions. And with that incisive observation, I'll shut my mouth.

The

CANDY KISS

Let's peer back into the mists of history in search of the origin of the kiss itself. Half hidden in the lush green leaves, we discern two creatures from the distant past—a mother and child. It looks like the adult is chewing her food into a pulpy mass and then transferring it into the infant's mouth. We avert our eyes from such a revolting act. Yet when that baby grows up, it incorporates the same procedure in its lovemaking. Gradually the transfer of food drops out of the ritual and lovers simply press their lips together. Such is the origin of modern kissing and the candy kiss itself.

As unappetizing as these anthropological facts are, knowing them can help you kiss more sensuously and erotically. The term "candy kiss" describes any kiss that contains something sweet in it, usually some candy that the lover passes directly to the mouth of his or her partner. It's a kiss for sensual lovers, requiring a sensitive palate and a willingness to overcome that initial disgust at the idea of sharing candy, food, or drink from your partner's mouth. Once you get used to it, you'll savor it like a good meal, and your kissing will become tremendously more erotic, stimulating, and satisfying. Take your time, come back for second and third helpings. Fill your diet with candy kisses and feast on the food of love.

Many lovers who practice the candy kiss are bashful and feel that they're doing something wrong. They may think they're slightly perverted or that their sex drives run in deviant ways, but actually they're quite normal, for deep down on some hidden level the candy kiss appeals to everyone. It is time to admit that one of the most delightful pleasures available to the lover is the taste of the partner's mouth.

Do you like the taste of your own mouth? If not, work to make sure that your breath is sweet and fresh and that your teeth are sparkling white. Flavor your mouth with mints so that your kisses will taste sweet. Do you like the taste of your partner's mouth? If not, suggest that he or she do something about it.

The *right* way to do the candy kiss

The candy kiss requires a sensual cast of mind. You may consider some of these instructions disgusting at first, but with time and practice this could become one of your favorite kisses.

1. Eat and drink things that color your tongue. If you drink grape juice, your tongue will become a weird shade of blue. The value of having a dyed tongue is that it acts as a stimulant and an allurement. The more interested your lover becomes in your mouth the more likely he or she is to want to kiss you. Most people are attracted to bright

red tongues. Red Kool-Aid is great for this. Experiment with various candies and drinks to see which ones will make your tongue change color, and ask your partner which color excites him or her the most. Show your partner your tongue in the same way you'd show it to a doctor. Say, *"Ah!"*

2. When you're eating candy, discuss its taste with your lover until your lover becomes very curious about it. Then show your lover what it looks like by opening your mouth. Don't overdo this, and do it only with hard candies—unless you know the other person *very*, very well.

3. Be observant. Study your lover's mouth the way Michelangelo would have studied a subject for a sculpture. When you're sitting in a restaurant let your eyes dart furtively at your lover's smile, at the lips, at the teeth. All these quick visual images are food for love. They will excite you, make your passion grow; they will ignite a keen and ardent desire within your heart. You will feel yourself powerfully compelled toward your lover. You will have hardly any appetite for good because you'll be so preoccupied with your lover's looks. When your partner laughs, let your eyes flick quickly to the interior of the mouth. Look at the tongue. Note the sparkling nectar that covers it. Such views will ignite a powerful thirst within you that can be quenched only by kissing—tasting—your lover's mouth.

4. Finally, pass candies from mouth to mouth. Some lovers like to pass chocolates, others prefer hard candy. There are hundreds of different candies you can use. Suck on the candy first, and then pass it, mouth-to-mouth, to your lover. Before long you'll both regress to a deliciously babyish state, eating from each other's mouth.

Tastes lovers hate

"I hate whiskey breath, and I refuse to kiss him when he smells like a barroom."

"When he eats Limburger cheese I tell him there'll be no kissing for at least two hours. As a result he's started on Muenster, which is mild and milky, and I don't mind it at all."

"When he smokes and wants to smooch—yuck! It feels like I'm kissing an ashtray."

"If he's brushed his teeth, I like his mouth. But I don't like his morning breath."

Tastes they love

"The thing about ice cream is that it cools her mouth down so that the kiss always starts off sweet and cold and then heats up as we get going. If we're eating ice cream cones, we like to kiss with a different flavor in each mouth. I know it sounds disgusting, but it really feels good to mix, for example, chocolate and vanilla flavors during the kiss."

"I like lemon kisses because her mouth gets all puckered up and my mouth sticks to hers. It sort of glues our lips together, and it feels good."

"Mint. It's fresh and tangy."

"We both love chocolate-covered dinner mints. We let our mouths get all minty, and when we kiss our tongues tingle. I don't always know whether the tingling comes from the mints or from the kisses."

"Around Christmas I get peppermint canes, which make

our mouths so sweet that we wind up kissing each other for a longer time. It's childish but lots of fun."

"Apple-flavored mouths make me dizzy. There's something sensual (and even sinful?) about the sound of your lover biting noisily into a fresh apple. The fragrance is stimulating and the taste of her mouth is so clean and bitter-sweet after she's eaten an apple that kissing her is like an aphrodisiac."

"I like the taste and feel of his mouth so much I sometimes think it would be nice to live in there."

"I love the taste of his mouth. Sometimes it feels small. His lips are smaller (thinner) than mine. After a year and half of kissing, I venture to say there have been only two times that I didn't like the taste of his mouth."

Do you ever eat food or candy from your lover's mouth?

MEN:
"Once in Paris this girl came up to me and kissed me and she had a mouth full of champagne and she spit it into my mouth and that was really nice. It was the first time anything like that had ever happened to me. That was one of my most memorable kissing experiences."

"We've held food between our lips or teeth to feed the other, to get that touching of lips that must occur when sharing food in this way."

"We pass ice cubes back and forth."

WOMEN:
"Yes—very exotic!"

"I love to kiss while drinking wine. Tasting the wine on my lover's tongue is wonderful!"

"Yes, especially cheesecake."

"We've sipped wine and passed candies. Not food, though; that's a bit disgusting."

"We pass gum back and forth."

"I like to exchange hard candy during a kiss."

"Almost every night after dinner I put a chocolate mint on my lips and make my lover grab for it. We always get a laugh out of this."

"My lover likes to chew ice cubes, and he's fond of sharing them with me."

The

SLIDING KISS

One survey response came from a fellow in his late twenties who said that when he was four years old his baby-sitter used to kiss him. She was a good friend of the family, almost like an aunt to him, and she baby-sat during the summer, usually wearing a sleeveless dress and watching television with him beside her. One day she asked him to kiss her, and he started kissing her face and mouth, which she liked. "But she wanted me to kiss her so much," he recalls, "that I had to think of some way to do *new* kisses because constant mouth and cheek kisses used to bore me, so I started to *slide* my mouth down her arms. She was rather chubby, and I enjoyed kissing the flesh of her arms. Then I'd slide my mouth all the way down to her hands and I'd kiss her hands. She thought it was a great game. I called it the sliding kiss."

He may have invented this one when he was four, but he's admittedly still at it. "I do the kiss with my lover now, and she likes it, too."

So go ahead and *sliiiiiiiiiiiiiide* all across her body. Be as risqué as you want. Slide down the neck and shoulders, and kiss along the way. *Sliiiiiiiiiiiiide* down her legs, too, stopping to put itty-bitty kisses on her teeny-weeny toes and then slipping and sliding all along her back. *Mmmmmmmmmmm, smmmoooooooch!*

Subtle sliding kisses

Once you perfect the longer slides (for example, down an entire arm), you're ready for the small, subtle variations. During a routine lip kiss, slowly slide your mouth from side to side. *What is this guy up to?* Take it nice and slow and savor your lover's mouth first from one angle, then from another.

The psychology of the sliding kiss

Some species, including horses and humans, regress to an earlier stage of development when making love, which is why lovers often call each other "baby." This fact can help you become a better sliding kisser. Don't think of kissing as a serious adult activity; instead think of it as a childish game. Study one-year-olds and you'll learn a lot about how oral a human can be. Were we *really* that way at one time in our development? More than that, on some deep level we're *still* that way; and when you get your lover to express this childish side, you'll succeed in unleashing his or her fullest erotic potential. So go ahead and *sliiiiiiiiiiiide*!

Places to slide-kiss

People like to be kissed in the darnedest places. Here are some suggestions from the survey. Slide to these spots and kiss:

- "I like to be kissed in the crook of the arm."
- "My shoulders!"
- "Between the fingers is nice. Toes too!"
- "I like being kissed directly in my armpit."

The

WET KISS

The typical mother of an infant deals with the most eye-opening dribble. If you've ever taken care of a baby, you know what I'm talking about. And let's be honest, it's not appetizing. The little boomer spits out chewed-up spinach or mysterious yellow mush, and then laughs until gobs of yellowish-white formula run over his lips and chin. The amazing thing is that . . . *the kid doesn't care*! To infants, stuff that comes out of the mouth is OKAY.

Now *that's* the attitude to adopt when you get down to serious wet kissing. You've got to let go of your adult inhibitions and revulsions from things in your own mouth and your lover's, and get back to a time when you loved that dribble. One way to do it is to act like a baby: They're so oral it's enough to make a Don Juan jealous. Another way is not to call it spit. Call it saliva. Better yet, make up your own pet name for it—mouth dew, nectar of the gods, tongue lubricant—or just say it differently: speeeet, honey, that's what it is, just some nice saleeeeva.

All right, now for the wet kiss, which comes in two flavors. The first has the saliva outside on the lips. People lick their lips when they see someone they'd like to kiss, so be flattered if your lover has wet lips. Try to develop a thirst for your partner's saliva and you'll be a more forgiving kisser.

The second type of wet kiss has the wetness inside, so to speak, and you'll encounter it during lip kisses of all types. This simply means that during a kiss you'll suddenly encounter a lot of wetness on and between your partner's lips. Be prepared for this and don't get put off by it. And as things heat up in a relationship, expect the kisses to get even wetter. Let your hair down, release your inhibitions. Wet kisses are OKAY!

Do you like both wet and dry kisses?

WOMEN:

"Wet much more than dry ones."

"Dry is better, but I like both."

"Dry kisses are fine for relatives and friends, or a quick peck good-bye at the parking lot when my husband and I leave for work. But wet kisses are best for lovers. Not sloppy ones, though!"

"Dry is better. A little moist is great, but soggy and wet is gross."

"Wet is better. But not sloppy. I don't like to be licked around the outside of my lips at all."

"I like dry initial kisses, but wet kisses later. Affectionate kisses shouldn't be too wet. Sexual kisses are wet."

MEN:

"Primarily dry, with just a touch of wetness."

"Yes, of course, better on the wet and slightly sloppy side."

"Wet are the best and we do make sweet water."

The

𝒰NDERWATER KISS

One of the most popular kisses with both sexes is the underwater kiss. Many men said they liked kissing in the shower, and almost all men questioned also liked kissing underwater in a pool or at the beach. Women also rated the underwater kiss a favorite. One young woman described her experiences kissing underwater around the world during her tenure as a Navy diver.

"As an ex-SEAL, I've kissed in the ocean and underwater with my SCUBA gear in Hawaii, Midway Island, Japan, the Philippine Islands, Guam, Australia, and off the coasts of Mexico and California. My lover and I learned to take a deep breath and leave the outlet lower than the valve to stop the compressed air and kiss underwater. With snorkeling it's even easier. You just spit out the mouthpiece and kiss underwater by making your mouth a bell jar."

How to kiss underwater

1. Take a deep breath.
2. Hold your breath and go under at the same time as your partner.

3. Open your eyes so that you can see how close you are.
4. You may want to hold on to each other so that you don't float apart. Maneuver yourself or pull yourself close to your partner's face and make lip contact.
5. Smooch away, occasionally exhaling air and spitting water out of your mouth when necessary.
6. Bring your lips together to end the kiss.
7. Resurface for air, and repeat.

Do you like to kiss underwater or in the ocean or pool or in the shower or bathtub?

WOMEN:

"I have a hard time breathing underwater, but I have tried it. In the ocean the waves break my concentration."

"Not underwater (yet . . . you've given me some ideas), but in a pool, yes. Chlorine is a little off-putting. Shower or bathtub, yes, but not for long as it's too arousing and leads to other things very quickly."

"Yes—underwater—it makes me laugh, so it's more of a game."

"I've never kissed underwater, but have kissed in the shower and in the ocean. Kissing in the shower is especially nice, with warm water running down your face."

"Only in a hot tub and shower. The hot tub was wild. The bubbles were everywhere, and so were the kisses."

"Kissing in the shower, with the water rushing down, mingles all the saliva and sweat together and makes things a lot smoother."

"Certainly in the shower. It can be very sweet with all

that wet. More men seem to find this thrilling, though, than I have.''

''I like to shower with my lover and wash his hair and then lean against the cold wall in the shower and kiss one of those long, slow kisses.''

MEN:
''Whenever I was on a date at the beach we did it. It's shorter because it's only while you hold your breath. Take a deep breath . . .''

''Taking a shower together and kissing sends shivers up my spine.''

''In the shower we love to hold one another, kissing and caressing the other's body.''

Remember to hold your breath!

T h e

Smacking Kiss

Late one night I awoke suddenly to strange sounds. *Squeak! Boing! Squeak! Eek! Eek! Boing-boing-boing! Squee-ee-ee-ee-ee-ee-ee-eek!* I peered from my bed in the dark at the air duct vent, which sometimes played strange jokes on us, wafting sounds from room to room. I was getting a very clear transmission from the couple who lived upstairs. *Boinnnnnnnng! Boinnng! Boing! Squeak! Squeak! Squeak!*

What the hell is going— I sat up in the darkness. Then I heard a woman's voice. "Oh," she was saying. "Oh-oh-oh-oh-oh." It didn't make any sense to me, and I began to curse the architects.

"Shut up!" I yelled. "Be quiet up there!" All to no avail.

Squee-ee-ee-ee-ee-ee-ee-ee-ee-eek! Boing! Boing! Boing! The sounds continued. And the woman was stuttering "OH!" faster than ever.

Suddenly it dawned on me, and I felt sheepish about having yelled at them.

But my neighbors didn't pay any attention to me anyway. They certainly didn't care who heard them, and neither should you. Whether it's the sounds of a bed squeaking or the lip-smacking sounds of kissing, the music of passion can be fun to make and hear. So, if you've ever been embarrassed or self-conscious about the little noises kisses make, forget it! Three out of four people surveyed actually enjoyed the natural sounds of lip-to-lip service and considered those smacking noises erotic and stimulating. One person in five also liked making little inarticulate *oohs* and *aahs* and hearing their partner make them too when in the middle of kissing. Some people like a natural kissing sound; others prefer a more exaggerated noise. Vary your style until you and your partner find the sounds you like best.

Do you like the noise kisses make?

WOMEN:

"I love the sounds of the mouth, teeth, tongue, and saliva, and also the noises emitted from us from being excited. They increase the intensity I bring into the kissing."

"I like the noise small intimate kisses make, but not big, hairy, slobbering smacks."

"Most of the time I like the noises, although they can be sloshy."

"I like the sounds of kissing, together with silence or nature in the background: the wind, birds, distant traffic, children playing, etc."

"Sometimes we make them on purpose."

"It's okay—not offensive. Sometimes we add weird little noises."

"If we're alone, the answer is a big YES—it's a turn-on."

"Yes, if they're incidental and not intentionally exaggerated."

"Yes, I love it. The noise is a great turn-on."

"I like the noise if it's *me* making it—I don't like listening to other couples."

The

$\mathcal{T}$EASING KISS

"Start with a really good kiss, then quickly pull away."

If you're in any kind of lasting relationship you'll want to make the teasing kiss part of every necking session. After a while kissing can get too serious, and even the most staid and stuffy lover will tell you there comes a time when you need to do something out of the ordinary to reduce the monotony that creeps into a repeated activity. The teasing kiss is a kisser's kiss, the one to turn to when all other kisses have been kissed, when your lips feel like cardboard and your tongue is tired and dry, when you're about to throw your hands up in despair and scream: "Kissing isn't all it's cracked up to be!" The teasing kiss introduces something out of the ordinary into overly serious necking. It's a playful kiss, one that will keep both of you alert and sensitive to each other's rhythms and spirit.

How to do the teasing kiss

1. Begin by kissing a few times so that you establish a rhythm of kisses to the point where your partner expects another one.

2. Break lip contact and wait for your partner to lean toward you for the next kiss.
3. Timing is important here. As your partner leans forward, you must lean forward also, *but don't allow your lips to touch.* The purpose of leaning forward is to draw your partner onward, to mislead him or her into thinking that another kiss is imminent.
4. Just before your mouths meet, lean back quickly, and just far enough so that your partner can't reach you with a kiss. Move with speed so that your lover is tricked.
5. If your partner smiles and gets feisty, you know you've done it right.

Do you ever tease your partner with a kiss?
Fewer men than women reported teasing with a kiss.

WOMEN:
"Sometimes I wait before returning a kiss. It's fun to play cat and mouse."

"Yes. He can be teased by my kissing his mouth and pulling away before he fully responds."

"I've teased and this can be very erotic. Once a man held me back from kissing him; he would kiss me and then wait quite a while before kissing me again. He prolonged our pleasure that way, hovering over me and sensing my excitement."

"I sometimes wait after he kisses me before returning the kiss just to see if he'll kiss me again if I wait. I do it to be pursued. But I usually don't want to wait."

"Yes, it's my favorite thing to do—aside from *being* teased."

"It all depends on the moment and mood. I'll return his kiss after a short wait (fifteen seconds), and I'll also wait as long as one minute; usually it's thirty seconds. During the longer waits we're looking at each other and touching our faces."

"Sure, I wait before returning a kiss. I think this is an unconscious understanding of how tension and excitement can best be built up."

"No. I generally find teasing dangerous. I teased a boy-friend once and he was offended by my change of behavior."

MEN:
"I get close enough, and then pull back before the kiss is given, to make my partner want to give it even more."

"Waiting before returning the kiss enhances sensitivity."

"Yes. I'll kiss her and then pull away so she can't kiss back, and repeat this until she gets frustrated. Then I give in."

Other kinds of teasing kisses

WOMEN:
"When your partner is asleep, sneak up on him and very gently rub your lips or fingers over his lips. It tickles something awful."

"When he's on the phone with his mother or with some-one from work, I like to kiss him and watch him wriggle!"

"I'll lick his lips very quickly with my tongue. I'll vary between his upper and lower lip, sweeping from one corner to the other and delivering quick pats with my tongue. If I kiss his ticklish areas, he'll start to fight and laugh at the same time . . . and become sexually excited. It drives him crazy. I do this on his stomach, chest, underarm, and inner thigh area."

"I tease him by just barely touching him with my lips, especially when I know he wants to kiss."

"I've teased him with a kiss because he wasn't interested in making love, or to make him think of me all day by kissing him passionately before he leaves for work."

"I always tease with kisses. I like to lick his lips or just brush my tongue over his lips, nose, and face."

"I like to tease him with kisses starting at his forehead and moving downward. I use light, gentle kisses that tickle and tingle a little. It drives him crazy!"

"Sometimes my husband stretches out his arms and moves quickly toward me, appearing to be running into my arms, but misses and continues past me."

MEN:
"I kiss her when I know she can't continue to kiss me, like when she's going out the door to work."

"I tease all the time when kissing!"

The

Counterkiss

I observed two lovers on a train trip recently. The young woman sat next to her companion, but by putting one knee up on the seat itself she was able to face him. She was good-looking, with intelligent eyes, and I wondered why she chose to sit in such a contorted position. When her boyfriend kissed her I discovered the answer. His kiss was a brief public kiss on the cheek. She gazed dreamily at him for a moment, then leaned forward and kissed him back, but she kissed him lower down on the cheek, almost under the ear. As if accepting an unspoken invitation, he returned the kiss. A few seconds later the young woman leaned forward and began to pepper him with quick little kisses on his cheeks and mouth. She was a classic counterkisser.

According to Ovid, *"Militiae species amor est"*—love is a kind of warfare. His comparison is liable to shock those who want to think of love as continual bliss and happiness, but his remark contains a real insight, one that will help you become a more adept kisser. He was referring to the fact that love often requires you to overcome obstacles before you reach your goal, in the same way soldiers must overcome obstacles in pursuit of victory.

But there is an even more fundamental similarity between love and war: Both depend upon similar tactics. One of the most essential tactics of warfare is the *counteroffensive*, in which one army strikes back at an invading force. When warfare is conducted on a one-to-one basis, as in boxing, this same tactic is known as the *counterpunch*, a punch you throw after your opponent has thrown a punch at you. In the sphere of love, the tactic is called the *counterkiss*, and it is executed after your partner has kissed you. Mastered fully, it enables you to interact with your lover perhaps better than any other kiss. The fundamental thing to keep in mind, though, is that a counterkiss is not a hostile act; while it is named after the counteroffensive, it is in reality an act of the deepest affection, tenderness, and love.

How to counterkiss

1. Be patient. Wait for your lover to kiss you. Only after you have been kissed do you go into action. A counterkiss is executed within a fraction of a second to as much as sixty or more seconds after you have been kissed. In effect it forms an *answer* to the kiss you received. You might think of it as setting up a nonverbal kissing dialogue between you and your partner.

2. Begin to think as soon as your lover kisses you. What is your lover feeling? Carefully and quickly size up your partner's mood by observing everything about the kiss you're receiving. The secret of giving good kisses is to be aware of the type of kisses you're getting so that you can give the appropriate ones in return. As one young woman advised, "*Listen* to how the other kisses you."

3. After your lover has kissed you, an invisible bond will

link your two hearts, a bond so powerful that it w
you irresistibly together. *But force yourself to pau:
you return the kiss.* If you withhold the expected ki
while, it can become a pleasantly tantalizing gam
to wait up to a minute or more before you kiss your lover
back. During this time smile at your partner, flirt with
your eyes, even have a conversation. The bond between
you will actually grow stronger because of the delay,
and you'll feel a lusty attraction drawing you together,
as if Cupid himself were whispering in your ear, "Return
the kiss . . . now!"

4. Kiss your lover back with a counterkiss that differs slightly
   from the kiss you received, for variety is the heart and
   soul of counterkissing.

Varying the counterkiss

Just as an accomplished speaker will introduce a new topic
into a conversation, an accomplished lover will change the
tempo, speed, duration, and other characteristics of a kiss.
Of course it's sometimes necessary and worthwhile to mimic
exactly the type of kiss you just received. For example, if
your lover is shy and kisses you with a little kiss, you can
wait ten seconds—as if you were shy too—and reply with a
timid kiss of your own. But more often than not you'll want
to introduce a subtle change in the kiss. This change in the
counterkiss will surprise and delight your partner. It's like
getting a love letter in the mail. The pulse quickens, the heart
is on alert, and all the senses are shifted to standby status. A
new move has been introduced into the kissing session. And
here is where the fun begins.

Varying the Tempo

When your lover kisses you slow, you should kiss him fast. When he kisses you fast, kiss him slow. It makes him think when you do something different. Sometimes he'll kiss you with short kisses, especially in the morning before work when his kiss may last only a second or two. But if you're in the mood for something more, kiss him back with a longer kiss. (See page 77 on the long kiss for pointers.) This may lead to an extended necking session so that you'll both be in danger of being late. That's the kind of send-off you'll remember all day.

According to our survey, some men have a habit of kissing their lovers with a series of quick little pecks. You may feel insulted at getting these perfunctory kisses, as if he were saying, "Take this, and take that!" Try letting more time elapse between your own kisses and pulling back when he attacks you with his machine-gun burst of short ones. Sometimes, though, you should kiss him back with the same rapid-fire kisses, which will throw him off guard and bring him around to taking you seriously and *kissing* you seriously.

Varying the Reply Time

Don't be afraid to tease the man you're dating by taking a long time to kiss him back. It's a wonderful form of flirting. (See page 67 on the teasing kiss for more details.) In addition to teasing and flirting, there are other reasons to wait before returning the kiss, as the following responses illustrate:

"I sometimes wait before returning the kiss. I do it to exchange looks and expressive mirroring. This has happened when we're six inches apart and my lover's face mirrors people I have known and loved; for example, mother, father, ex-boyfriends, etc.''

"I sometimes wait before returning a kiss in order to savor his kiss, or to smile at him, or to look at him to say, 'I love you.' "

"Occasionally I like to wait a little while before returning his kiss, because I like to look at him and maybe lick his nose."

Varying the Selfishness

Let's admit it . . . some kisses are more selfish than others. Sure, it's great to be caring and sensitive, but not *all* the time. Sometimes you'll feel like kissing ruthlessly, not caring how your partner feels, while other times you'll want to kiss sensitively, giving pleasure as best you can and letting your partner take his or her fill. Don't be surprised if your partner is turned on by your aggressiveness and selfishness. One woman said that the sexiest kiss she ever got was from her boyfriend, a police officer, who kissed her ruthlessly in the police station men's room as if he were out to satisfy only himself; he kissed her with a hunger and passion she said she remembers even ten years afterward.

Varying the Style

Try these suggestions to add diversity to your counterkissing:

• If your lover kisses you with one type of kiss exclusively, reply with a different type. If you're getting dry kisses, give back wet ones. If your partner is kissing you with closed-mouth kisses, put some tongue into it. (Study page 121 on the French kiss for details.)

- If your partner keeps his hands at his sides, hold and cuddle him.
- If he starts with light kisses, initiate deeper ones with your tongue.
- If he gets very intense, you may have to lighten it up with quicker, dryer kisses. But usually things develop from the less intense to the more intense.
- Read one or two sections from this book about new kisses you'd like to try. And then remember to put the ideas into practice when you're together. Little by little you'll add diversity and style to your counterkissing. Your lover will be pleasantly surprised, and so will you.

The

$\mathcal{L}$ONG KISS

Once upon a time there was a beautiful princess who vowed that she would marry only if a suitor's kiss convinced her that he was the perfect match. Hearing this, the king issued a proclamation stating that his daughter would marry the first man whose kiss she truly enjoyed, but in order to dissuade frivolous attempts he added that all who failed to please her would be put to death immediately.

Soon men from all over the country flocked to the palace, and each one was led into the chamber of the princess and allowed to kiss her once. She thought the man who kissed her forehead was too timid. The man who kissed her hand was too formal; the man who kissed her foot, too ridiculous; the man who put his tongue into her mouth, too bold. And all of them were executed.

In desperation the king sent messengers to the far reaches of the kingdom, seeking more men with new types of kisses. Next morning a very ugly old man was first on line. When he came into her chamber, the princess was horrified and sat back on her bed, thinking, "No matter what his kiss is like, I will reject him."

The old man stepped boldly forward and kissed her. His

kiss lasted such a long time that the princess began to get dizzy. She wished he would stop because she was breathless and her head was swimming and she felt a strange tension in her nerves. And then suddenly she felt as if she could breathe again, yet he was still kissing her. The kiss seemed to last for hours. Her senses were numb, and all she felt now was the kiss, burning into her blood like a slow fire. She could hear the voices of the other men outside her room, but she made no move to stop the kiss, for something had begun to warm her heart, and she was kissing him back passionately; yet it never occurred to her that she was breathing naturally through her nose. Finally the door flew open and all the princes and dukes rushed in.

The old man stepped back quickly, covering his face with his hood.

"You've been in here an entire morning," the other men complained.

"Now ask the princess for her answer," the old man said.

The princess was surprised, for something in her heart prompted her to speak, and without thinking she heard herself saying:

"He is the one I will marry."

The crowd stood back in shock. And at this the old man threw off his hood and was miraculously transformed into a handsome young prince. Everyone gasped in wonder. Tears of happiness came to the princess's eyes. And true to her word, she married him the next day, and they lived happily ever after.

The moral of the story is simple: Kiss the long kiss and you will be transformed. It is a potent weapon in the war of love because it brings you close to your lover for an extended time, during which you two are almost one person, breathing together. There is something about the kiss that does strange and marvelous things to people.

How to perfect the long kiss in six easy steps

1. Kiss your lover squarely on the lips. You must begin with the basics, and a good solid kiss is the foundation of the long kiss.
2. Hold the kiss tightly so that your lips are in contact all around. This ensures that you have a good seal on each other's mouths.
3. Prolong the kiss until you feel somewhat breathless. Part of the fun of this kiss comes from the slight feeling of breathlessness that occurs at the outset.
4. Now breathe in through your nose. This step is the trickiest. If you find it impossible to breathe through your nose, you'll have to break off the kiss and start again at step one. Practice breathing through your nose during the day, keeping your mouth closed and inhaling and exhaling through your nose only. Keep practicing until you can breathe through your nose for an entire minute without opening your mouth.
5. Listen for the sound of your lover's breathing. This is another joy of the breathless kiss. Since the two of you are breathing through your noses during the kiss, you'll be able to hear each other's breath and you'll get some sense of each other's emotional state.
6. When necessary, swallow, but don't break lip contact. In this way you can prolong the kiss for many minutes without interruption.

Dos and don'ts of the long kiss

Do:

- Snuggle and cuddle during the kiss.
- Be passive at times and merely keep your lips in contact with your lover's lips. In other words, simply stand together with your lips touching. Although this may *sound* dull, I guarantee that it will make your day! You will feel the keenest electric shocks coursing through your nerves and all up and down your body.
- Get used to kissing for long periods of time. This kiss offers a unique opportunity for uninterrupted and constant mouth-to-mouth contact with your lover.
- Combine this kiss with the French kiss and other types of kisses. One of the benefits of learning the long kiss is that it can be combined with virtually every other kiss. And by combining the technique with other kisses you can prolong your favorite types of kisses indefinitely.
- Like the chimpanzees described in Chapter 1, make little panting noises now and then.

Don't:

- Don't panic. Some people get anxious during long kisses because they feel they're suffocating. Just remember to breathe through your nose and your panic will subside.
- Don't try the kiss if you have a cold or allergy. If your sinuses are congested and your nose clogged, you won't be able to breathe through your nose.
- Don't hyperventilate. Some people get so excited that they begin to breathe rapidly. This excess breathing introduces too much oxygen into the bloodstream and can make you dizzy. Relax and enjoy the kiss and breathe normally through the nose.
- Don't gasp for air when you break lip contact.

The longest kiss listed in *The Guinness Book of World Records* lasted an amazing 417 hours. Although you needn't set a world record, keep in mind that longer kisses are generally more erotic than shorter ones. Your lover will be delighted when he finds that what he expected to be a short kiss turns out to be a long, deep one instead. And if you can kiss for four or five minutes straight, you're doing better than 95 percent of your friends and neighbors. Survey results reveal that most people kiss for only a minute before breaking lip contact.

How long do your longest kisses last?

MEN:
"Anywhere from a peck to a few minutes on end."

"About forty-five to sixty seconds. Usually seven to ten seconds."

"I guess it could go for a minute, one nice long kiss."

"A couple of minutes."

"Three minutes."

"A long time."

WOMEN:
"Until I run out of breath."

"My longest kiss lasted about one-half to three-quarters of an hour. That was with my first boyfriend. I like kisses over one minute long."

"Maybe a minute?—as long as I can breathe and there's some variation. Actually I'd probably prefer running a lot of kisses together."

"My longest kisses last four to five minutes. I love long kisses! The length of a kiss depends on the type of kiss and our moods. The kisses range from pecks (one second) to French kisses (four to five minutes). I tend to do more French kissing, and these are longer-lasting for me than closed-mouth kisses. I'd say the average length of a kiss is twenty-five seconds."

"Usually two or three minutes per kiss. I like them to last as long as possible."

Long kissing sessions

In addition to long kisses, many people love long kissing sessions. Also known as necking sessions or simply making out, the length of such activities can vary widely. Some people get bored rather easily with kissing, perhaps because they don't know many different types of kisses. By becoming familiar with the different kisses in this book, however, you'll be able to lengthen your necking sessions so that they last entire afternoons, entire evenings, entire dates. Ah, what bliss! What unending, excruciating joy!

WOMEN:
"In my opinion, you're wasting your time if you don't kiss for at least twenty minutes."

"Sometimes kissing (just kissing) lasts for an hour or two and continues through making love. Other times my lover and I will kiss all night and save making love for the morning."

"Ten to fifteen minutes is an easy stretch—fully clothed. But naked it is less. I like long kisses in places where you cannot *do* anything else."

"We seldom kiss for long periods of time—usually two minutes—and kissing doesn't always lead to sex. We often kiss with our clothes on, but both definitely prefer to kiss with our clothes off."

"I usually engage in kissing for only about from two to five minutes with my husband before we have sex."

"I don't know how long, but I know I love to 'make out' for hours."

"I like to kiss for thirty minutes to an hour or so."

"I have had marathon kissing sessions—like four hours—not one continuous kiss, but a very intense session. I enjoy this as long as it doesn't get routine."

"Sometimes we kiss for hours."

"It depends so much on the circumstances. If you're making love, you can kiss continuously for hours."

"Usually the kissing lasts (a) just a few seconds in passion, (b) less than a minute when we're more involved but don't have much time, or (c) mostly all the way through lovemaking: fifteen to twenty minutes."

"Some kisses have started all-night kissing sessions. One friend and I started kissing at 9 P.M., and we kissed all night until 3 A.M."

"One time I kissed a friend for approximately seven hours—no foreplay, just fun kisses. It was excellent!"

The

$\mathcal{P}$UBLIC KISS

They pass by and look and sometimes they even stop and stare and then they move on again. And all the while you hardly notice them because you've wandered off in your mind to a place where the palm fronds are always swaying in the breeze and the kisses are always sweet. These people who pass by while you kiss in public don't bother you at all; they're like shadows on a hot summer day when you haven't got a care in the world. The crowd seems to melt into the background, and all that's left is this delicious sensation as you and your lover kiss on a busy sidewalk, at a shopping mall, or on the beach.

The public kiss is very popular in the United States, where about 90 percent of respondents said they've enjoyed doing it. It's apparently even more popular in Europe. According to one young woman, "We should approach kissing the way the Europeans or French do. French girls many times do oral kisses in public on the *rue* or square or park. Nothing is ever thought about it." Survey responses from people who've been to France confirm that there is in fact more public kissing there than anywhere else in the world.

Kissing in public requires only a modest bit of courage.

Usually no one interferes, although passersby may glance over to see what you're doing.

There are lots of good reasons for kissing in public. Here are just a few:

- You simply can't wait to get somewhere private.
- You're saying good-bye at a train station or airport.
- You enjoy being affectionate and you don't care who sees.
- You're at a party and other people are necking, so you get turned on to the idea and do it too.
- You're an exhibitionist at heart and like to have an audience for your kissing.

How to kiss in public

1. Make sure you're standing in a place where people won't bump into you. The two best places to stand on a sidewalk are up close to a building or right at the curb.
2. Take a quick glance at the surrounding crowd to make sure no one's about to walk into you.
3. Step close to your partner.
4. If your partner doesn't look immediately receptive to a kiss, say something to let him or her know what you're going to do. In a crowded bowling alley one December, a young woman told a boy, who was wearing green pants and a red hooded jacket, that she wanted to kiss him because he had on Christmas colors. Then she kissed him in front of everyone.
5. Kiss your partner boldly and without shame.

Things to avoid in giving a public kiss

- Don't do it to excess so that other people feel uncomfortable.
- Don't get paranoid.
- Don't make an announcement to the crowd.
- Don't excuse yourself. Why should you? Virtually everyone kisses in public at some time or other.
- Don't grin and gawk at passersby after the kiss. If people look at you, simply ignore them. They may be picking up important pointers for use in their own public kisses.

Do you ever kiss in public?

WOMEN:

"I'm not timid about showing affection in public, and it's fun to get caught. Sometimes I feel a bit like a show-off, sometimes special, sometimes embarrassed. I watch for my husband's reaction."

"Yes, I do kiss in public. One time my boyfriend came to pick me up from work. He rushed over to me and proceeded to kiss me. I gave him a peck. He wanted a longer kiss and I let him know I didn't want to. My boss was in the room. It was a very informal work setting, yet I was still uncomfortable. I generally like pecks in public, although I do have fantasies about kissing him passionately in public. Passionate kissing is very private for me. I'll kiss passionately in a car or if I'm sure no one else is looking."

"Before I emigrated to the United States from France, I'd kiss in public at parties, and I felt great."

"I prefer discreet, quick kisses."

"Not very often because kissing in public limits what you can do."

"A particular man finally grabbed me in a restaurant (while we were enjoying a glass of wine and the tension between us) and kissed me very passionately. I was embarrassed *and* extremely excited. What was exciting was that his passion overrode any sense of his surroundings."

"Nothing more than quick hello kisses. If I want anything else, then I want intimacy, and that needs privacy. I don't appreciate watching others neck, either."

"In public places, but not in public (with the exception of kissing the groom). I felt excited to steal a kiss in a public place—clandestine kisses are very exciting."

"I've grown up disliking other people's PDAs (public displays of affection), so I don't do it myself. On occasion I'll give a short kiss."

"I was leaving for three months on a trip to France to work. My husband, who was my boyfriend at the time, was with me at the airport to say good-bye. He wore sunglasses to hide his teary eyes. We had a long, romantic kiss before I left. The feeling lingered a long time afterward. The day after I returned he proposed!"

"I was brought up never to show *any* affection in public. But I have kissed in public anyway."

"I wouldn't want to make an exhibition in a public place. But if you were meeting your lover after a lapse of time, for example, at an airport, it would be completely natural to kiss intimately and openly. I always enjoy being kissed in public.

I come from England where we kiss instead of shaking hands."

"We never clinch kiss in public, but we give each other pecks all the time."

MEN:

"Indulging on the dance floor (while dancing, that is) during a slow dance is . . . yum."

"On the beach. It felt good."

"I kiss in public any time she wants me to or lets me, but I still have to be careful. She doesn't like people to see her kissing me."

"I have kissed in public. Usually the girl is a little bit more embarrassed, but I guess it could be the other way around. I never paid any attention to the people in the area, never noticed whether they stopped and stared. I don't generally mind if I see other people kissing in public. When I was in France I saw a lot more of it."

The wedding kiss

Your first kiss as husband and wife may be the most important public kiss you'll ever do. Hundreds of people, scores of photographers, and the eyes of history may be upon you at that moment. No need to worry or lose your nerve. Take a quick look at the crowd, then kiss with these pointers in mind:

• Make it a kiss for you and the guests who are watching. The kiss should last a long time; you want to give the photographers a chance to check the exposure and click away. Meanwhile you're kissing away.

- Men, don't be afraid to lean her back, Hollywood style.
- Women, lean back like Scarlett O'Hara for a full photo.
- Choose the spot for the first kiss beforehand.
- No French kissing—it doesn't show up on film and there isn't enough time to get warmed up for a French kiss.

"It wasn't memorable," said one nineteen-year-old newlywed. "He kissed me as we were leaving the church, and there was nothing particularly romantic about it."

Many people said that their first kiss as husband and wife took place in a most uninteresting setting. To remedy this, arrange for a romantic place that you'll remember for years to come. Try to have a professional photographer on hand to capture the moment. And make it a long, deep, soulful kiss that expresses all your feelings.

One woman who had her wedding kiss recorded on film said, "That photo summarized everything we felt for each other and has become almost a yardstick to measure all our subsequent kisses."

There's one thing about the public kiss that I saved for last, and I recommend that you share this with your lover. Brain researchers assure us that things sexual make a more vivid and enduring impression on memory than do ordinary events. If this is true, then the public kiss offers a unique opportunity to take mental *snapshots* of places you've visited. Each public kiss should imprint upon your memory everything about your lover, the setting, and your mood, illuminating the highlights of all your romantic activities. You may even want to plan these kisses ahead like a photographer setting up a shoot. Arrange to meet outdoors some night at a sidewalk café, or at the edge of the road overlooking ships coming into a harbor, or one spring evening on top of a mountain at sunset when birds are winging overhead and other lovers are enjoying a picnic. And when you're there together, ignore the crowd and simply . . . kiss! Your partner will never forget it, and neither will you.

The

$\mathcal{M}$USIC KISS

Molly is twenty-two years old, and she wears a walkwoman (that's what she calls it) when she kisses, because she kisses . . . to music. She's outside the library this afternoon waiting for her boyfriend Richard, and she's listening through earphones to loud rock 'n' roll. When she spots his crew cut over the crowd of students, her heart begins to pound like a tom-tom, and she turns the volume down but not off to hear him say hello. Then they're alone behind the library surrounded by all the green of summer, and the music fills her ears again.

In the inky glass doors she sees the reflection of her yellow radio clipped to her shorts. With one hand she changes the channel, recognizing snippets of lyrics, passing classical and pop stations, until she locks in on a love song that was very popular a few years ago, one with a strong beat, so that when she puts both hands around Richard's waist she's kissing to that love song. She watches the red reflection of his shirt blend into the blond reflection of her legs in the glass as she kisses him. Richard is such a sweet guy, and he kisses so divinely, his lips tender and soft and exploring. And as the music becomes more insistent, he rocks her back and forth in his arms, kissing her with long breathless kisses that send shocks one after another over her body and through her blood until she's numb with a fainting feeling all through her nerves and through the extremities of her limbs. And then the music starts pounding in her ears, a new song about true love that she likes, and it takes her up and away, and she rises on her toes to snuggle into Richard's kiss, going further and further into him as if drawn inward by the beating rhythm, lovely Richard with his crew cut and his sweet kisses that never seem to end—oh, how they blend into the music and make you go inside yourself and then outside yourself to that never-never land. She falls into the kiss like a rock sinking deeper and deeper into a bottomless pool until she's blind and unconscious and transformed somehow so that she knows that even when the song ends and she blinks open her eyes, she's not going to be the same, she might not even be Molly anymore. Some part of her will always be lost in that kiss, lost in a fathomless pool from the bottom of which Richard is calling to her—Richard and the music together calling from the unseen depths.

The music kiss can unleash emotions, make you feel romantic and sexy, and evoke moods you thought you'd never feel again. It requires being aware of how music can affect your mood, and then letting the mood evoked by the music influence the sensation of the kiss. Whether it's blues or rock on a walkman, jazz or classical on a stereo, or country music on a car radio, many lovers reported that they liked to listen to music while kissing.

MEN:
"I like to kiss with background classical music. It's very pleasurable (if neither Bartok nor Ives)."

"Listening to music on a walkman while kissing is like going to a Pink Floyd concert."

"I like kissing while listening to slow love songs on a walkman."

"The only problems with kissing while wearing a walkman are that the wires get in the way and you can't hear what your partner says."

WOMEN:
"Yes, it can be a lot of fun and very sensual if it's the right kind of music, with crescendos."

"Sometimes you can kiss harder when there's a loud drumbeat."

"I like to kiss to Gloria Estafan in my kitchen!"

"Soft, sensual jazz vocals are good."

"When kissing I especially like slow and sensual music, or fast and throbbing, or sweet and melodic, or sentimental. Or any kind."

"I listen to music when kissing in the car."

"Every once in a while my husband and I will kid around and move our tongues in each other's mouth to the music we're listening to."

"Sometimes cuddling and kissing to soft music before bed is nice, as well as kissing to music while dancing."

"Music may create a mood where before there wasn't one. And this mood may lead to kissing."

"Kissing with a walkman is great because you have more

desire, more emotions, you feel excited because you have the music inside; you feel inspired.''

"I kissed once with a walkman on and it was distracting. When my boyfriend had the same song on as me it was nice; but then we changed channels and I was listening to a love song and he was listening to heavy metal and it was weird.''

"It can be very romantic if both people with the walkman are listening to classical music.''

"I think it's great to listen to the radio when you kiss, but a walkman is rude.''

The

COUNTING KISS

One of our respondents, a man in his late twenties, used to love to kiss his girlfriend so much that she would get tired of it, and as a result whenever they went on dates he was afraid she'd tell him to *stop* kissing her. "I had an insatiable appetite for kisses," he says, "and I was constantly trying to figure out ways to get her to kiss me for longer periods of time." One of the methods he used was the counting kiss. And if you're in the same situation—if you love to kiss more than your partner does—you can use this kiss to get more kisses and extend your kissing time.

How to do the counting kiss

1. Wait until you sense that your lover is getting tired of kissing.
2. Determine how many more kisses you'd like to give her.
3. Quickly look around the room, simultaneously searching your memory for significant dates or numbers (the age of your lover, a famous date from history, the number of

her street address, the first three digits of her phone number, and so on).

4. Tell your lover that you're going to give her X number of kisses, linking the number X to the number you found in the room or in your memory for significant dates or numbers.

5. Proceed to kiss her to your heart's content, counting silently to yourself as you go along.

6. Kiss the first few kisses quickly so that she thinks you're going to get through them all in a short time.

7. Announce the number periodically, say every tenth kiss. "That's ten, my dear! . . . Twenty! . . . That's thirty kisses down, and seventy more to go! . . . Forty, my love; patience, please! . . ." and so on.

8. After the first quick burst of kisses you can slow down the speed of your kissing and enjoy yourself.

Here's an example of how it's done. When the gentleman mentioned at the outset of this chapter was kissing his girlfriend one afternoon, he felt that she was getting bored, but he wanted to kiss her about a hundred more times so he started to search his memory and look around the room for numbers. She had recently had her twenty-second birthday, and he could have told her he was going to give her twenty-two kisses in honor of that, but it wasn't a high enough number. Then he noticed that they were listening to a radio station with a frequency of 105, so he told her he would give her 105 kisses in honor of the station they were listening to. She didn't believe he could give her 105 kisses, and it became an enjoyable little contest between them. In this way he prolonged a kissing session that would otherwise have ended before he was fully satisfied. Try it!

The

SURPRISE KISS

Remember how Hannibal used the tactic of surprise to defeat the Romans? He crossed the Alps in the winter of 218 B.C. on elephants! The defenders were so surprised they suffered a stunning defeat at the hands of the great strategist. So too will your sweetheart, not expecting your surprise kiss, fall like the Romans at Cannae, and in the battle of love victory will be yours. Inscribe within your heart the motto, "I am the Hannibal of lovers," and you'll surmount any obstacles to romance, for fully 85 percent of men and 98 percent of women love surprise kisses.

How to give a surprise kiss

1. Wait for the right time. Just as Hannibal attacked when no one believed he could, so should you deliver your kiss when she doesn't expect it: early one morning, when other people are present, or maybe when you're shopping together.
2. Surprise your lover in a place where you usually don't kiss.
3. Use tactical distractions to enhance the surprise. Tell her she has nice earrings and then, while pretending to examine them, plant kisses on her neck and shoulder.

4. Endure whatever hazardous conditions are necessary to get into position to deliver the kiss. If you have to travel through rain and snow and dark of night to sneak up on her as she leaves work—then do it!

Do you ever like to surprise (or be surprised by) your lover with a kiss?

WOMEN:

"I like to surprise and be surprised with a kiss. It's an unexpected yet welcomed show of affection. I feel special."

"Yes, I love both. I'll come up behind my boyfriend and kiss him on the neck and cheek. I've also done this and had this done to me during the middle of a conversation."

"Although I hate surprises in general, to be kissed for no apparent reason other than because you want to at that moment is nice—but it should be quick."

"When the relationship is new, it's hard to know when the next kiss is coming. An old boyfriend kissed me quickly when he was introducing me to his friends for the first time. That made me feel so wonderful inside."

"Yes, sometimes I think he's not thinking of me, and then he'll come in and kiss me."

"One day I was in a clothing store alone. My lover walked up behind me and surprised me with a kiss on the back of my neck. It's still memorable after ten years."

"It's nice to be kissed unexpectedly when I'm lying in the sun on the beach. Or when I'm half-asleep and my husband wants to get me awake to make love."

"In the gym my lover walked across a crowded room of women and kissed me passionately while I was trying to do leg presses. He returned coolly to his weights. I continued exercising, but my heart was thumping like a machine gun."

"I love when he comes up behind me when I'm working in the kitchen and starts kissing me on the back of my neck."

"Yes—anytime, anywhere—magic. . . ."

"I absolutely *love* to come up to people I love from behind and give them a bear hug and kiss on the neck or cheek! I also love to wake up (or be woken up by) my lover with a kiss."

MEN:
"Yes, when you least expect it because it's crowded or not the typical time or place for a kiss."

"Yes, to say 'I love you' while dancing."

"Yes, just to catch her by surprise and see how she responds."

"Yes, first thing in the morning to wake my mate up—starting slow on the toes, or elsewhere, and ending on the lips."

"Yes, on the nape of the neck, usually. But softly on the lips as well."

"When you can't resist the temptation!"

"Yes, especially a gentle kiss behind the ears or upon the neck."

The

$\mathcal{V}$ACUUM KISS

Imagine that you're sitting with your boyfriend on the couch, but neither of you are watching television. You're wearing a new silk blouse, and he's told you three times this evening that you look stunning. Finally he leans forward to kiss you. After a few minutes you're necking seriously, and you begin a long kiss, during which your lips adhere tightly to his. Slowly and playfully and without even thinking about what you're doing, you begin to suck the air out of his mouth. What a feeling! His lips taste like the inside of a peach, and as you draw his breath deep into your lungs you can feel your souls mingling. Then he begins to suck the air out of your mouth, and by the time you've given him every atom of breath you have, you feel like you're so totally and completely his that your nerves are vibrating with shameless excitation. You've let him take your very life's breath away! How together you are at last! How mystically close! And on some level how profane and wicked it feels! Like Hylas in the pond with the nymphs, once you've acquired a taste for vacuum kisses, they'll take you deeper and deeper beneath the surface until you're lost in all their myriad charm.

Types of vacuum kisses

In a double vacuum kiss you keep your lips sealed tightly together as you both suck the air out of each other's mouths simultaneously. Your cheeks may actually hurt from the intense pressure exerted on them. During this version you may also suck your partner's tongue; anything in his or her mouth is fair game to vacuum into yours. With the possible exception of the French kiss (see page 121) the sealed-lip vacuum kiss will link you more closely to your lover than any other kiss. After all, it involves sharing your air—the very essence of life. If you can combine the French kiss with the vacuum kiss . . . well, one shudders at the possibilities.

In the reverse vacuum kiss, you just touch your lips together—no tongue or teeth involved—and blow back and forth into each other's mouth.

In the mouth-to-mouth vacuum kiss you hold your partner's nose and then blow air into his lungs as if you were resuscitating him.

Do you ever suck air out of your partner's mouth?

WOMEN:
"I hold his nose and blow air into his mouth so that it fills his lungs."

"Only someone I really know well."

"I've been married one year, and I do this once in a great while. Sucking air out of your lover's mouth seems to be something done by new lovers, who tend to experiment more."

"Yes, he hates this."

"Yes! I also return the air. Sometimes it's only our lips touching—no tongue or teeth involved, and we're blowing back and forth into each other's mouth."

"It was an unusual experience to have my tongue almost sucked out of my head. Now I can't make up my mind whether it was good or bad because it's really both. At first you may not enjoy your tongue being sucked in such a forceful manner, but afterward your tongue will be left vibrating with a tingling sensation that's rather pleasant."

"It's not fun at all when done with a lot of force. But when done gently it can be enjoyable."

"It feels weird, but I like it. It takes quite a bit of practice."

MEN:
"It's very exciting to have this done to you."

"It's such a turn-on. It's like she's giving herself totally to me when we suck air back and forth, and I can't think. I just love it."

"The vacuum kiss is a must! You simply suck the air out of your partner's mouth and watch them make a funny face."

"I hate when someone sucks the air out of my mouth. You can also blow air into someone's mouth. It kind of hurts but it's funny."

"It's different but sexually arousing. The partner who receives the kiss gets a blast of air in the beginning until the person runs out of air. Then it's a warm mist."

The

𝒫ERFUME KISS

Chances are you've encountered this one on your own without even knowing it; perhaps like this . . .

In the afternoon sunlight you check your curls in the mirror as you wait for your nails to dry. You're wearing blue cotton pants, a topaz-yellow blouse, white sneakers, and matching yellow socks. You notice the time and run into your big sister's room and ask her frantically if she has any perfume you can borrow. She points to a little amber-colored bottle with a label written in a foreign language. She's talking as you splash it on hurriedly without even time to smell it or listen to her, and then you move.

You're out the door and halfway to the street, where Tommy's car is parked, before the scent catches up with you. Hold on! It rises to your nose in slow, insistent waves and you suddenly know you used too much. But you can't do anything about it now. *What did she say? It's a French perfume and it's stronger* . . . Then you're sitting beside him; he's driving to your favorite picnic spot, and even though the windows are down you're constantly aware of this woodsy floral scent. What *was* that stuff? When he parks, the fragrance fills the whole car, and you're mortified even as you notice that this smell has layers to it, luscious woodsy notes on top, and beneath them a heavy musky fragrance that lingers like the refrain of a sad song. Tommy kisses you, and as he does the odor seems to change, giving the impression that the air contains something like talcum powder. He inhales deeply, saying you smell delectable, delicious, sexy, naughty. And indeed you do. Suddenly you give yourself over to his kiss, and the fragrance which at first seemed merely musky now becomes pungent; almost imperceptibly the odor begins to resemble the emanations that rise from day-old underclothes. He's kissing you with a steamy passion, and your senses are numbed as layer after layer of the intoxicating fragrance fills your nostrils and penetrates deep into your lungs. Your sister never prepared you for this! He kisses more insistently than ever, his lips wandering deep into the hollow of your neck, seeking the source of that deliciously intimate aroma.

So goes the perfume kiss, *a kiss in which any sensual odor plays a part*. But this is merely the start. It's a kiss with as many subtle variations as there are fragrances. Still, of the thousands of fragrances you can perceive, perhaps none is as exciting as the smell of your lover's hair or arms or neck. Indeed, throughout history the most passionate lovers have been those most sensitive to human smells. The Emperor Napoleon loved the unwashed smell of his wife so much that he would write to her from the battlefield and tell her not to bathe for a week so that when he got home he could enjoy her natural body odor. When the poet Goethe traveled, he took along his lover's bodice to be reminded of her scent. And when one of H. G. Wells's mistresses was asked what she liked about the overweight, unattractive writer, she said he smelled of honey.

Many survey respondents said that the smell of their lover

was often the greatest natural aphrodisiac, more powerful than any perfume. It's no surprise that perfumers often try to duplicate human smells and regularly use animal scents like skunk, civet, and musk to give a sexual tinge to their creations. Even some vegetable scents are sexually stimulating; the smell of yeast, baked bread, beer, fresh tobacco, cut grass—all act as mild aphrodisiacs, reproducing as they do some natural human scents.

Unfortunately, the majority of smells are anathema to modern society. It's even difficult to talk about the subject since our language has no words for most of the smells you can perceive. When you're told every day by advertisers that you must deodorize yourself and eradicate all body odors, you begin to get the message that natural smells are bad. So you'll probably have to coax yourself and your lover into trying the perfume kiss.

How to do the perfume kiss

1. If your lover is wearing perfume, breathe it in deeply before, during, and after each kiss.
2. Embrace your lover and inhale the natural fragrance of the hair, the sweat, the flesh itself.
3. Kiss all up and down your lover's body, stopping at any interesting smells along the way. Be fearless about encountering strong smells, but if you come across a smell you don't like, simply move on to the next.
4. When you reach a smell you *do* like, tell you lover! And keep on kissing.

Do you enjoy kissing a person who is wearing perfume?
MEN:
"Yes, when perfume is delicate, not overpowering."

"Yes, it adds another dimension. If the perfume is strong it repels me. If it's just enough to detect, and only here and there, it adds to a person's natural scent, which I usually enjoy."

"I love the way she smells! When I kiss her sometimes I'm like a hound dog, sniffing and kissing all over her body, and getting turned on as I come across different odors, whether natural or artificial. I especially love smelling under her arms. Sometimes when she's going away for a while she'll let me borrow one of her undershirts so I can be reminded of her by its odor. And I hate when she uses a deodorant. It kills all her sexy smell."

"Her perfume sort of puts me in a daze. Soft and light is just great."

WOMEN:
"I enjoy my husband's natural body odor."

"Perfume can increase my *intensity* and the type of kiss I deliver. It's exciting to move around the body and stop at a smell. This also applies to natural body odor. I have a very sensitive nose."

"I love kissing someone who's wearing fragrance."

"The smell of cologne can help stimulate arousal, but it normally *tastes* lousy."

"A faded cologne on a man can be very pleasurable. It

must be faded, though. It has to be blended into his own scent, which hopefully is great.''

''For me, kissing is a five-senses type of thing, and kissing a man who is wearing a good cologne is so exciting.''

''I don't really like deodorants, talc, aftershave. The smell of a clean man is more than enough to drive me wild.''

''Even when he isn't around and I smell that cologne, I always smile.''

The

$\mathcal{R}$OLE-PLAYING KISS

Imagine that you're Cleopatra kissing Caesar in the great palace at Alexandria. Exotic incense wafts through the royal bedchambers, morning sunlight streams down from the high windows, and the silk sheets await you and the ruler of the Roman Empire. What kisses you could kiss if you were king and queen of the Nile!

Or imagine you're a widow living in the Old West, and you're standing outside the bank on a hot afternoon. Suddenly a man on a black horse rides up in a swirl of dust. A moment later you're on the horse beside him. Now the two of you are galloping out of town. Your friends and neighbors stand staring in the street. The scent of leather and gunpowder fills your nostrils. The horse slows down and finally you're alone with your secret lover—the outlaw from Dodge City. You get off the horse and the man takes you by the hand and leads you under a tree. You look up into his eyes in the shadow of his black hat. With a sardonic sneer on his lips he takes you into his arms. No words are needed. You know what you're there for. No one can see the two of you now. But even if the world were looking, you couldn't stop yourself. Your heart is beating fast. The sun feels warm on the back of your neck. Yesterday is gone. Tomorrow doesn't matter. All that matters is what's in your heart, and that tells you to do only one thing.

Kiss him!

Kiss him and forget everything else. Kiss him as if you would die for him. Kiss him as if your blood and his were running together through your lips.

But kiss him!

Everyone has yearned to be someone else, if only in dreams or daydreams. In role-playing, these fantasies somehow free your creative and emotional side, bringing fire and passion into kisses that would otherwise feel ordinary and dull. A role-playing kiss is any kiss in which one or both parties make believe they're someone else by introducing an element of pretense into the situation.

There's no limit to the different kisses and scenes you can develop. Don't worry about losing your mind or becoming someone else permanently. When the kisses stop and the dust clears, when the gold tables and silver jewelry vanish, when the FBI stops following your car, you'll be yourself again, same as usual—with only one difference: you'll have kissed a kiss the likes of which no one has experienced for hundreds, maybe thousands of years. Here are just a few of the role-playing kisses you can try:

Slave and master

WOMEN:
"We pretend to be slave and master sometimes."

"This is something I haven't done, but I may try it with a suitable partner."

"I've done this, but not recently. It's a lot of fun, but tends to push buttons!"

"There were occasions when I *felt* like a slave to someone. This giving-in can be luscious. But maybe, sadly, it's not pretend enough."

MEN:
"No, I don't like that—but she likes to have me be forceful and be a real man."

"Sometimes we adopt exaggerated dominant and submissive roles, telling the other, 'Talk dirty to me,' or demanding that the other reply, 'Yes, sir!' or 'Yes, ma'am!' "

Prostitute and customer

WOMEN:
"I pretend to be a prostitute or stripper every now and then. The kisses that follow are usually a little more aggressive or deeper."

"I haven't done this yet—maybe in the future."

"I pretend I'm a prostitute sometimes in my fantasies."

The androgynous kiss

If you're like 99 percent of the people I surveyed, you're going to resist this one. The androgynous kiss can cause intense anxiety in most people because Western society rigidly prescribes the sex roles each of us adopts as we grow up. But if you're brave enough to try it, you'll discover at the end something more valuable than any other kiss can offer, for when done properly the androgynous kiss provides the keenest insight into your lover and lets you understand him or her better than any other kiss in the book.

How to do an androgynous kiss

1. You don't have to have a sex change operation or wear different clothes or cut your hair to do the androgynous kiss. All you have to do is think differently. First relax and imagine yourself a member of the opposite sex. How do you feel? I told you it wasn't easy. This is the most difficult step, and if you find yourself thinking, "This is silly," that's a natural first reaction. But it's an essential step, so you may want to work on it for a few days, silently, mentally, and bit by bit you'll get the hang of it.

2. This kiss can be accomplished without telling your partner what is going through your mind. After all, your lover will never be able to read you thoughts, so he or she will never know. But if you do tell your partner what you're doing, it's not necessary for your partner to make a switch too; the androgynous kiss can be accomplished by one person making the switch mentally.

3. In kissing your partner, imagine what it would be like to be a person of the opposite sex. By doing this, you'll be reclaiming parts of your psyche that you may have denied or never developed before. For example, some women report that they feel a surge of energy when they imagine that they're a man. Some men feel that they gain added sensitivity and emotional depth when they switch sex roles in their mind.

This kiss and the concept behind it make some people very nervous. Most men left this question blank. Perhaps they were frightened by the concept. Women were somewhat more receptive, although some expressed shock and outright criticism of the notion of androgyny.

Do you ever pretend to switch sex roles while kissing?
MEN:
"No!"

"Sometimes I'm active (dominant) and sometimes passive (submissive) in my sexual moves toward my lover, and this varies, depending on the time and mood I'm in."

"Pretend? No. But there are plenty of role reversals! I enjoy being pursued, having the other take the lead, as much as I enjoy pursuing. I feel a relationship has to be give-and-take. So sometimes she's in charge and doing the work and giving me pleasure, and other times I do the work, give direction, etc."

WOMEN:
"Yes—but this really requires trust—and is very challenging. Sometimes it's just in my head."

"I've wondered what it would be like to be a man kissing *me*. I've wondered this because I'd like to know if I'm a good kisser."

"No. I feel that both parties can be as giving and taking and passive and aggressive as they want to."

"Being *responsive* is what's important—being able to sense the other's desire."

"No. I don't see there being a male or female way to kiss. I've kissed both women and men. I've applied intense pressure and in the next moment have given light, feathery kisses."

"I've tried to imagine I'm a man kissing a woman. Is that sick or what! . . . I've got the supposed upper hand—taking control of the kiss, handling the hair, jaw, etc. It's good."

The gangster kiss

It is early morning, and you and your lover are standing on the sidewalk outside the bank. The streets are almost deserted. You have one hand in your jacket pocket on your .38 automatic. At the curb Vito is sitting in a black Ford with the motor running; he's smoking a cigarette to calm his nerves. Your partner is looking up at the tall glass buildings that mirror the blue sky. You turn to her and notice a strange romantic gleam in her eyes. Perhaps it's only the reflection of the bank. She takes a breath to bolster her courage, and her white teeth flash. Without thinking you bend down and kiss her roughly on the lips. Suddenly her mouth feels like the softest and most beautiful thing in the world. Your heart is beating fast, your head is swirling, and you almost forget that in a few minutes you'll either be rich or dead. . . . You have just succumbed to the gangster kiss.

Because gangsters live outside the law, they're not hampered by rules and restrictions; they live the way they want to and enjoy a greater degree of freedom than most people. Their methods of kissing can teach you how to have fun and feel free. And since they often risk their lives, gangsters are usually filled with a high-strung anticipation and nervousness that can overflow into their sex lives and make their kissing urgent and erotic. They know they may be dead tomorrow, and as a result they routinely kiss with a fervor that would sear the lips of the lawful.

How to kiss like a gangster

Keep in mind that you don't have to break the law or actually become a gangster in order to enjoy the unparalleled passion of the gangster kiss. Just follow these seven simple suggestions:

1. Use your imagination the way you did when you played cops and robbers.
2. Think like a gangster. It may not be easy at first, but with a little practice you can develop the thought patterns of a criminal. After all, aren't lovers somewhat like gangsters? Gangsters have nicknames (like Charles "Pretty Boy" Floyd, and George "Machine Gun" Kelly), just as lovers have pet names for one another. The toughest gangsters are quick to defend each other and often die together. So too will true lovers defend one another against the slanders and accusations of the world. Gangsters share the fruits of bank robberies and holdups, just as lovers share their financial resources and earnings. And deep down, gangster loyalty is really another kind of love, similar to the love that men and women feel for each other.
3. Act like a gangster. Look over your shoulder all the time. Are any federal agents following you? Go places that gangsters would go. Stroll with your lover through the financial district, walking up and down in front of large banks and casing them like a professional.

4. Dress like a gangster. Wear a jacket and tie if you're a man, a long dress if you're a woman. Wear diamond or fake-diamond jewelry. Begin to talk like a gangster, too. If you've finished a meal in a restaurant and are ready to go, instead of saying, "Are you ready to leave?" say things like, "Let's scram." If you notice someone walking behind you, tell your partner, "The feds are on our tail." All this gangster talk will get you in the mood for gangster love.

5. When you go out with your lover, make believe that the FBI is trying to find you. This will bring you closer together. You'll feel it's the two of you against the world. Let's say you're sitting in a small restaurant. Tell your partner to watch the door. Lean over the table and whisper to your lover as if you were afraid a federal agent might be sitting at a nearby table. When you look at your lover imagine that this is the last time you'll see him or her. Savor every moment. And when you get an opportunity, lean across the table and kiss. Love isn't like this every day. Not everyone has to love on the run. The element of danger, mystery, and suspense will make your kisses come alive.

6. Gangsters are more ruthless and coldhearted than most people. As a result their kisses are often rougher and more aggressive. When they kiss they do it for their own pleasure, not really caring about the person they're kissing. So kiss your partner roughly now and then, thinking only about your own pleasure. Kiss your lover's lips the way you'd eat an apple, with an aggressive, almost biting attack. It helps to have a sneer on your lips as you pull back and survey your partner's mouth for another bruising kiss.

7. When you're alone with your lover remember the furtive love of Bonnie and Clyde. One afternoon they were neck-

ing on the sofa in an apartment they had rented in Texas when they were surprised by Dallas police officers who arrested Clyde for a robbery he had committed in a nearby city. But before the arrest the two killers were kissing the gangster kiss. Like hunted animals they lived their lives trying to avoid capture. Think of how passionately Bonnie would have kissed Clyde under such circumstances. Then kiss your lover in the same way. Stolen kisses were never this good!

Do you ever make believe that you are criminals?

WOMEN:

"I enjoy making believe my husband is a crime boss. I bought him a gray felt hat, the kind you see bank robbers wearing in 1930s movies. He doesn't smoke, but I get him to pretend to light a cigarette and then look up and discover me. I tell him to say rough things to me, like, 'Hey, honey, I ain't seen you around here before,' and I take him to gangster movies so that he can learn how to act. Then afterward we go out to a restaurant and try to stay in character as criminals, but it's difficult when the waiter comes to our table. Usually we'll both crack up laughing, and the waiter just looks at us funny. After the restaurant we'll go outside and try to kiss like criminals. What's most fun about it is that we can be rougher with each other because our kisses are somewhat playacted when we imagine that we're kissing a killer. It makes it erotic."

"I once went out with a guy who was into making believe we were different couples, like Napoleon and Josephine, and kings and queens, and once we pretended we were Bonnie and Clyde. He even made me call him Clyde. He started talking funny, as if he had a limited mental capacity. Then before we went out—we were going dancing—he made believe he couldn't find his gun and he had me searching all around my own apartment for his supposedly lost gun. Finally he told me it would be a big risk to go out without a gun, and he held me in his arms and kissed me. He said, 'Baby, we may not come back alive.' I was laughing, but when he kissed me it was exciting.''

"Once at a costume party I dressed up as Al Capone, and it was fun. When I kissed my boyfriend I laughed right in his face.''

"The more aggressive you pretend to be the more passionate the kissing becomes.''

"I pretend to be Madonna because she has a rebellious attitude. Sometimes I dress and act outrageously like she does.''

"I sometimes make believe I'm the gangster's woman and I wear a really trashy dress. My boyfriend acts rough, and it's an escape from the civilized world for me. No domesticated man can compete with him when he's that way.''

MEN:
"Once I tried to convince my girlfriend to make believe she was a criminal, but she refused. I told her it was only a game, but she wouldn't do it, so I gave up. A few weeks later I went to her house, and she was wearing a long black dress and red lipstick and perfume, and she started talking like a moll. I got so turned on I couldn't believe it. When I kissed her, she kept acting like a gangster's girlfriend, and I couldn't get enough of her. She's usually very meek and passive, but she kissed me hard and aggressively this time. I think that

little session of playing the moll liberated something deep and passionate in both of us.''

"I make believe I'm a gangster, and it's a weird power play. The kisses become short and violent.''

"I imagine myself sometimes as some sort of gangster, easing off my Harley-Davidson, wearing a black leather jacket. I have a stern look on my face. Then I bury my face into hers for about five seconds, and then I hastily look away, holding one arm around her waist. No words are exchanged—this is very important.''

The gangster kiss is by far the most creative type of kiss. It demands both a killer's ruthlessness and a lover's sensitivity. It is one of the most formidable weapons in Cupid's arsenal, and once you master its subtle intermixture of fact and fantasy, your love life will never be the same. Every meeting with your lover will be as memorable as a blackmail threat, every date as exciting as a conspiracy, every kiss as stimulating as a bank robbery.

PART THREE

Kisses from Around the World

The

ℱRENCH KISS

The French kiss is the most intimate, sensual, and exciting kiss, and yet up to this time there have been no explicit descriptions of it for lovers to study. Young people interested in the French kiss, also known as the soul kiss or tongue kiss, have had to rely upon chance or luck in perfecting it. Typically lovers stumble upon the kiss accidentally while on a date. It might happen this way. . . .

You are sitting with your sweetheart on the couch. You had planned to take in a movie, but after her parents go out for the evening, she suddenly suggests that you stay inside. She picks up a book of love poetry and wonders what you think of a certain poem by Tennyson. You lean over to read the poem. Suddenly you are sitting right next to her. The poem is entitled "Kisses." You look down at the page and begin:

> *Once he drew*
> *With one long kiss my whole soul through*
> *My lips, as the sunlight drinketh dew.*

You are just about to kiss her when she takes the initiative by moving forward to kiss you. What a pleasant surprise!

You yield to her, becoming passive for a moment as she leads the way. You are so torpid, so easy, so yielding that as she presses her mouth against yours, your lips slowly part and her tongue slips inside your mouth for a moment. Now she is perhaps a bit shocked, and she draws back.

"We better stop for a while," she says.

"No, no."

Now you kiss her, and as you do her lips open and your tongue slides lightly and effortlessly into the soft interior of her mouth. You can hear her breathing. You have forgotten to breathe yourself. Finally you remember to inhale through your nose so that you can prolong the kiss. Your heart is pounding and you feel you have broken through to new territory—and indeed you have. You think you have been perhaps too aggressive. But your fears are allayed when you feel her tongue meet yours. Her mouth feels and tastes so delicious as your tongues twist about each other. And now her tongue pushes slowly and deeply into your mouth. She is so bold, almost brazen in her exploration.

There are no words that can adequately describe the sensation of the French kiss. Suffice it to say that you have now reached an advanced stage of kissing that can lead to almost symbiotic closeness with your lover. Handle this kiss with care and it will pay you rich dividends. You and your lover will get to know each other in a new and intimate way, for the French kiss can bring you closer together than even the act of sex.

Her family was expected back in two hours. Can you believe it, here they come now! How can it be? Have two hours slipped by so quickly? Your heart is still beating fast as the two of you move slightly apart. But you feel that you are still in contact with her. Somehow the French kiss has brought you so close together that for hours and days afterward you will feel different toward each other. It's as if a mystical connection links the two of you together. Ah, the delight of it! Ah, the secret thrill!

Do you like French kissing?

WOMEN:
Almost all women (96 percent) said they enjoyed the French kiss.

"When I think of French kissing, one man in particular comes to mind. His French kisses weren't sloppy or overly wet. They were penetrating. He used to play chase with his tongue and my tongue in such a way that I wanted it to never stop."

"Very much—you feel like you're melting into each other."

"I like the speed, depth, unification with the other."

MEN LIKE IT TOO
"The more tongue the better!"

"I like deep, fast, hard tongue kisses."

"The French kiss I could do for hours. I place one hand on the girl's lower back and the other by the side of her head and play with her hair. I breathe with my nose and playfully stick my tongue in and out of her mouth, licking her lips and sucking the air out of her mouth."

"I don't enjoy wide-open wet exploring. I like to French with the mouth only slightly open and prefer a softer, more gently probing kiss."

"When I was first kissed this way, I felt, in some sense, violated. I didn't want anybody putting anything of theirs in anything of mine! If I'd been asked, I would've been more receptive; but I wasn't, and it seemed a bit gross. After a few times, and some weeks, I got the hang of it, but it's not my favorite form. I do enjoy having someone run her tongue along the sides of my teeth, up around the gums. I don't enjoy the stabbing, penetrating, rigid-tongued kiss. I like the fooling-around kind of kiss; a little dance kind of kissing."

Women's advice for men

Many women said that although they liked the French kiss, they found that men resorted to it too often, were too unimaginative (didn't move their tongues enough), or were too aggressive (initiating French kissing too early in a relationship). Their advice for men: (1) go slower, (2) don't French on the first—or even the second or third—date, (3) be gentle, (4) try to sense your partner's mood and respond in kind.

"Men seem not to know any other way to kiss. It can be okay at times, but not *every* time."

"The most challenging things are how to get someone to allow you to show them how to kiss (nobody wants to be told they don't know how!) and how to get some finesse into Frenching."

"I don't like a lot of tongue. I really hate kissing someone for the first time and having their tongue go down my throat."

"I'm Irish/English, and until I was thirty I didn't know

or enjoy this French kissing. I finally learned it from an American man. If I'm in love, French kissing is heaven on earth. If not, it's kind of playing with each other's mouth.''

"I like French kissing if it's soft, sensual, and intimate; as long as it's not slobbering or deep throat. Gentle, delicate French kisses deepen intimacy."

"I like it but not when I feel suffocated by the person's tongue. I like light French kissing."

"Sometimes it's invasive if you're not in a serious or long-time relationship."

"If the other person just wiggles his tongue it's no good. There needs to be passion and sensuality. I hate being sucked or swallowed by kissing."

Other comments

One woman told us that she thought her mouth was unraveling the first time her boyfriend's tongue entered her mouth. She couldn't believe what she was feeling. It was so sensual, so intimate, so expressive.

Many people reported that French kissing was their favorite type of kiss. One enthusiast said that she does face and tongue exercises so that she can French kiss for longer periods of time. She actually trains for it like an athlete. A good exercise is eating mashed potatoes, she claims, because they have the texture and consistency of the inside of someone's mouth.

Another woman said she likes tongue kissing after she and her lover eat candy because his mouth tastes sweet and delicious.

A young woman from California explained that she and her boyfriend go on nature walks in the woods and when no one's looking they stop and kiss. She said that when he puts his tongue in her mouth she forgets everything else, losing contact with the world and getting caught up in the sensation of the kiss.

Dos and don'ts of French kissing

Although the French kiss has been around for centuries (the term itself came into the English language in 1923), there are dozens of variations and always plenty of excuses for experimenting with the basics. Here are pointers that will help you perfect the French kiss:

Do:
- Use your tongue.
- Take an active part in the kiss. Push your tongue into your partner's mouth. It may feel funny at first, but you'll get over your shyness in no time.
- Take a passive part at times. When your partner pushes his or her tongue into your mouth, relax and enjoy the sensation, meeting him or her with your tongue.
- Breathe through your nose so that you can prolong the kiss.
- Close your eyes now and then so that you can concentrate on the feelings.
- Utter little inarticulate cries and moans to communicate some of your excitement to your partner.
- Explore the roof of your partner's mouth, as well as the inside of the cheeks, the teeth, the region under the tongue, and the palatoglossal arch at the side of the back of the

mouth. Your main interest, of course, will be your partner's tongue because it will feel so sinfully soft and will respond to your every move and touch.

DON'T:
- Don't be afraid of tongue contact. Some lovers get shy when they encounter their partner's tongue. You must overcome this bashfulness.
- Don't press your lips together tightly, because this makes the French kiss impossible.
- Don't gag.
- Don't get nervous if you feel your head swimming and your nerves tingling. It happens to the most experienced lovers during the French kiss.
- Don't chew gum. Gum will only interfere with the kiss and with the sensations you will feel. Besides, gum doesn't feel as good as the inside of your lover's mouth, does it? If you do this kiss properly, with an empty mouth, you'll feel that your soul is merging with your lover's soul. Would you want to spoil that sensation with a wad of chewing gum? Nay, nay!
- Don't overdo it. Many people report that they like French kissing so much that they do it for an hour or more nonstop. But, as with anything else, too much of a good thing can be counterproductive. If you tongue-kiss for an hour without stopping you're bound to decrease your pleasure. The solution is to take a short break every five or ten minutes. Chat with your partner. You might talk about the kiss itself. Have a glass of water or some candy. There's nothing like a French kiss between a peppermint-flavored tongue and a cherry Life Saver–flavored mouth! As you can see, the combinations are endless.

The

$\mathcal{E}$SKIMO KISS

Three teenage girls are chatting in the freezing cold evening outside a small wooden bakery in Barrow, Alaska. The sign over the door says "DONUTS AND COFFEE." A boy rides up, drops his bicycle in the snow, and goes into the bakery with one of the girls. As soon as they enter they stand toe-to-toe and begin to rub noses.

A good-looking young woman sets out from the village of Igloolik for a day of seal hunting in the Canadian Arctic, climbing into a small motorboat with her baby strapped to her back. She turns to smile at her husband, who has trudged through the snow to see her off. As she starts the motor, he leans forward and they press their noses together.

The wedding is over, and the newlyweds turn to each other. Ritual drums echo across Canada's Great Slave Lake in the dusky mist as the two lovers rub noses in a prolonged embrace.

These vignettes illustrate an important but little-understood custom known as the Eskimo or nose-rubbing kiss. The kiss is popular not only throughout the Arctic regions, but also among the Maoris of New Zealand, the Society and Sandwich Islanders, the Tongans, and most of the Malayan races (which is why it is alternately known as the Malay kiss). The kiss is also practiced in Africa and is the predominant form of kissing in Asia. Actually the kiss involves more than simply rubbing noses, as the following instructions demonstrate:

How to do the Eskimo kiss

1. Begin to embrace your partner.
2. Simultaneously bring your faces close.
3. Aim your nose slightly to one side of your lover's nose.
4. When your noses make contact, let them slide along each other.
5. As soon as the tip of your nose reaches your partner's cheek, breathe in through your nose, savoring the fragrance of your lover as you do.
6. Lower your eyelids.
7. Smack your lips in a kissing gesture, but don't actually kiss your partner's cheeks; instead kiss air.
8. Inhale through your mouth as you kiss the air, enjoying the delicious perfume of your lover.
9. Move your nose back and forth slightly, sliding it along the side of your lover's nose.
10. Now and then bump the *tips* of your noses together. Smile and gaze into your lover's eyes while you do this.
11. Occasionally bump the *sides* of your noses together as a variation on the sliding motion that predominates in the kiss.

Variations on the Eskimo kiss

A number of variations on the basic Eskimo kiss have been noted by anthropologists. Darwin described a Malay kiss in which the initiator of the kiss places his or her nose at right angles on the nose of the partner and then rubs it, the entire kiss lasting no longer than a handshake. Cook described a South Sea Islands variety as a brisk mutual rubbing with the end of the nose. Still others have described an Australian variety which consists merely of face rubbing. In many tribes the lover simply pushes his or her mouth and nose against the partner's cheek and then inhales.

The Eskimo kiss compared to the nose kiss

Keep in mind that the Eskimo kiss differs from the nose kiss (see page 38) in the manner of execution. During the Eskimo kiss you simply rub noses together without kissing the nose with your lips, but in a nose kiss you actually kiss your lover's nose with your lips. The only time the lips are used in the Eskimo kiss is when you kiss air to the side of your lover's cheek. In contrast, during a nose kiss your lips are constantly in use, kissing the entire length of your partner's nose. From this comparison it should be clear that the Eskimo kiss and the nose kiss can be executed in sequence. After kissing your partner's nose with your lips, rub your own nose along your partner's nose. With all this attention directed to your partner's nose, you're sure to get some reaction, if only a sneeze or a laugh.

Do you ever rub noses?

WOMEN:
"Yes, a little now and again."

"Only with a child. It seems like a childish thing to do."

"I used to when I was a kid. We thought it was funny."

"I don't really care for it, but I've done it."

MEN:
"I like to *bump* noses."

"Rubbing noses works best when you simply want to hug her and keep your faces close."

About three in four people said they rubbed noses, yet not many made detailed comments on this kiss. As any anthropologist will tell you, people aren't very open to the cultural practices of those in other societies. Unfortunately, we're probably denying ourselves a very excellent kiss by not doing this one more often. Nose rubbing can be an exotic way to get close. As some of the comments bring out, however, you'll have to get over your feeling that it's childish, or learn to enjoy the childish fun of the Eskimo kiss.

The

JAPANESE KISS

The Japanese, who are generally very discreet in their personal habits, are rather shy about kissing. They don't really like the custom. They don't even like to talk about the subject. Parents and children never kiss in Japan. Lovers sometimes kiss, but almost always it's as a prelude to intercourse.

One young woman from Japan said, "Since coming to America, I have tried to learn American customs, including kissing. I said to my husband, 'Why don't we try to become more like Americans and kiss more?' He got indignant and refused. 'I'm Japanese,' he said, 'not American.' So we don't kiss much. Back in Japan my mother would drop dead if she saw two people kissing in public—really no one kisses in public. She'll immediately turn off the television if the actors kiss."

Here, then, is my full report on the art of the Japanese kiss:

How to do the Japanese kiss

1. Be shy about kissing.
2. Forget what you already know about it.

3. Ignore everything in this book.
4. Stand at least a foot away from your lover.
5. Lean forward.
6. Don't hug or embrace.
7. Don't use your hands at all.
8. Gently touch your closed lips to the lower lip of your lover.
9. Don't say anything.
10. Don't laugh.
11. Be very serious.
12. Act slightly embarrassed about the whole thing.
13. Keep your lips pressed to your partner's for a while, but don't expect any reaction and don't expect to be kissed back.
14. Break off and step back.
15. Be discreet and say nothing about the kiss.

"What good is the Japanese kiss?" I can hear some readers asking themselves. "It's so . . . *sexless!*"

Far from it! Strange as it may seem, the Japanese kiss is one of the most erotic kisses in the book. The element of holding back, of hesitancy, of Taoist simplicity—all this has its arousing effect. After you've been kissing for a number of years you're liable to become jaded. Nothing seems new anymore. Kissing loses its zing, its excitement, its stimulating qualities. But this is largely because you have been trying always to progress, when instead perhaps it is time to regress, to forget, to become the neophyte for a while . . . and kiss as the Japanese do.

The
CONTINENTAL KISS

Europeans kiss with a passion and fervor that would make the brashest Hollywood stars blush. But there's no magic to their technique. You can easily learn the methods they use. If you really take the advice in this chapter, your kisses will have the same sensual and steamy quality that lovers from France, Portugal, Spain, Germany, Italy, Greece, and Scandinavia boast about to the rest of the world.

Two men from Italy introduced me to the Continental kissing style one afternoon after I asked them for information about how European kissing was unique. They began to talk about kissing, and they showed me a greeting kiss done all over Europe, first demonstrating the kiss with each other, then demonstrating it with a young woman who happened to walk out of a restaurant. (They even attempted to demonstrate the kiss with me right on the street.) The greeting is popular in most of Europe and is executed as follows:

The Continental greeting kiss

1. Shake hands.
2. Move closer and embrace.

3. Hug affectionately, patting each other on the back.
4. Kiss each other, first on one cheek, then on the other.
5. Talk during the kiss, saying things like, "Good to see you!" and "How are you?"
6. Continue kissing, alternating from side to side as you talk and hug.

The Continental greeting kiss should be modified if you want to do it in a romantic setting, since the original intent of the kiss is merely to greet someone, not to make love. But this modification is easily accomplished: Next time you notice that you're standing to one side of your partner during a kiss, break off and shift position, kissing the other side of your lover's face and embracing from a different angle. In this way the fundamental moves of the Continental kiss (kissing first on one cheek, then on the other) will add just the change of stimulus needed to make the embrace sexier. Of course, you can use the technique as a greeting as well, especially if you're in the habit of kissing your lover when you meet. By including some elements of the Continental style you'll make your greeting kisses sensual and expressive.

Another greeting kiss popular in Europe—especially in Poland—is the hand kiss. In Warsaw, men kiss the hands of women when they meet in the same way that people in other countries shake hands. In places where the hand kiss serves as a normal and expected greeting, no one considers it a sexual act; it's seen as an expression of respect, not love. But in countries where the hand kiss is unusual, it will be perceived as the *ultimate* sensual greeting kiss. Do it like this:

The Continental hand kiss

1. Take the woman's hand in yours and hold it so that the back of her hand faces your mouth.
2. Either raise her hand to your lips or, for an even greater show of respect, lower your lips to her hand.
3. Kiss the hand gently, with a kiss neither noisy nor moist.
4. If you wish to be more ceremonial and perfunctory, merely make a kissing gesture without touching your lips to her fingers.
5. If you want to convey a special degree of respect or admiration, apply relatively more pressure with your lips when you kiss the hand.

In addition to these Continental greeting kisses, Europeans vary key aspects of the traditional lip kiss to make their kissing more erotic and passionate. Here's how they do it, and how you can do it, too.

How to kiss Continental style

1. Begin in a leisurely and easygoing manner, executing the first few kisses casually.
2. Ignore the clock by telling yourself that you're only going to kiss your partner once or twice. After your first few kisses, talk or simply sit together without kissing for a while. Then pick up where you left off, with a few more casual kisses.
3. Kissing sessions should last two to three times longer than you're used to.
4. Kiss all over the body, and linger over each part of the body that you kiss. Imagine that your lover's lips are

candies and suck on them until you can taste their sweetness.

5. If standing, get close, but don't stand toe-to-toe; instead, put your leg between your lover's legs. If sitting, the woman can put her legs over the man's. The more contorted your positions, the more Continental and erotic your kisses will become.

5. Vary your kissing style unexpectedly. For example, suck hard, bite, do a sliding kiss, a nose kiss, an eye kiss, an ear kiss, and a lip kiss in quick succession.

7. The most important element of Continental kissing involves your motivation. Forget about doing anything else with your lover, and especially forget about ********. Try to make love simply by kissing. With that as your goal, you'll have the proper mind-set for this fervent and steamy kissing style.

What to say during the Continental kiss

While kissing Continental style, sprinkle your love talk with terms from other languages—or even from slang—to give your chitchat a cosmopolitan and worldly flavor. Our language has a number of unusual terms for kissing, including *necking*, *smooching*, *spooning* (a colloquial term in the United States and also in British slang, perhaps derived from the fact that people who kiss often stand and fit together like two spoons), *bussing* (a word derived from the Old French *baisier*, to kiss), *smacking*, *osculating* (a technical-sounding Latinate term), and *sparking* (a colloquial term). The following list of foreign words and phrases will help you appear worldly and urbane to your partner, especially if you pronounce them with a sensuous accent.

FRENCH
embrasse-moi (ahm-BRAHS-mwah), a polite "Kiss me!"
le baiser (luh BAY-zay), the vulgar term for "kiss"
baise-moi (base-mwah), a vulgar "Kiss me!" This is also a rude way to say let's have sex.

SPANISH
el beso (el BAY-so), the kiss
besar (BAY-sar), the polite way to say "to kiss"
besame (BAY-sa-mee), the polite way to say, "Kiss me!"
grajeo (gra-HAY-oh), the slang term for "to kiss"
grajeame (gra-HAY-a-mee), the slang phrase for "Kiss me!"

ITALIAN
il bàcio (eel BOT-show), the kiss

SWEDISH
kyss (chiss), a kiss
kyssa (chissa), to kiss
kysstäck (chiss-tek), kissable, perfectly sweet

GERMAN
kus (rhymes with English *puss),* a kiss
Abschiedskuss (AP-sheets-kus), a farewell kiss
Bruderkuss (BREW-duh-kus), a friendly kiss
Doppelkuss (DAWP-ul-kus), two kisses in quick succession
Morgenkuss, a morning kiss
Versöhnungskuss (fer-ZUR-nungs-kus), a reconciliation kiss, a make-up kiss

How to use the list

When you're close to your lover, whisper phrases such as the following:

—Let's buss on the bus.
—Osculate me! (You might get slapped if you say this with the wrong tone of voice, so be careful.)
—Come on, honey, let's spoon.
—Less talking, more smooching!

You and your lover can have your own private code language to use in talking about kissing in public if you remember some of the terms from foreign languages. While on line to see a movie, for example, say: "You're so *kysstäck*, as soon as we get inside, let's start *Doppelkussing*."

The

𝒯ROBRIAND

ISLANDS KISS

Here's a kiss your lover has probably never heard of—a kiss named after the South Sea Islands where it's so commonplace that everyone does it. The kiss was unknown in the rest of the world until 1929 when anthropologist Bronislaw Malinowski visited the Trobriand Islands (pronounced: TROW-bree-ahnd), investigated their bizarre sexual customs, and wrote a marvelous account of his research, *The Sexual Life of Savages*.

The Trobriand Islands are located about 1,850 miles due north of Sydney, Australia, in that part of the South Pacific Ocean known as the Solomon Sea. Natives of the islands are dark-skinned and belong to the Paupo-Melanesian race. Malinowski studied every aspect of their sexual life, from premarital intercourse to marriage to pregnancy and childbirth to lovemaking and the erotic life. His research is highly respected, and his work ranks close to Darwin's in the realm of cultural studies.

Malinowski found that the Trobriand natives consider our custom of kissing (pressing lips to lips) a rather silly and dull practice. But although they don't kiss as we define kissing, they do use the mouth during lovemaking. Two lovers will typically begin by talking for a long time, grooming each other's hair, and hugging and caressing each other. Then they rub noses just like the Eskimos. They also rub their *cheeks* together and they rub mouth against mouth—without kissing. Next they suck each other's tongues in a sort of variation on the French kiss. When things heat up, they begin to rub tongue against tongue. Next—and this is the crucial step—they bite and suck each other's lower lip until the lip bleeds, and then they bite off each other's eyelashes. This biting off of eyelashes is done during orgasm as well as during the earlier parts of lovemaking. They also exchange saliva from mouth to mouth and bite each other's chin, cheeks, and nose. During more intense moments they also pull so forcefully on each other's hair that they often tear handfuls of it right from their lover's head! Such is the nature of kissing among the Trobriand Islanders.

For those brave souls willing to try something new, the instructions for the Trobriand Islands kiss follow. You needn't do each and every step. Skip around and try whichever ones interest you.

How to do the Trobriand Islands kiss

1. Begin by getting close. Sit on a mat together.
2. Have a conversation.
3. Hug and caress.
4. Run your hands through your lover's hair.
5. Rub noses.
6. Rub cheek against cheek.
7. Rub your mouths together—without kissing!
8. Suck each other's tongues.

9. *Rub* tongue against tongue.
10. Suck your lover's lower lip *vigorously*.
11. Bite your lover's lower lip until it bleeds.
12. Exchange saliva from mouth to mouth.
13. Bite your partner's chin.
14. Bite your partner's cheek.
15. Nip at your partner's nose with your teeth.
16. Thrust your hands into your partner's hair and pull forcefully.
17. Bite off the tips of your lover's eyelashes.

Probably the most unusual part of the kiss is the biting of the eyelashes. (According to Malinowski, everyone in the Trobriand Islands has eyelashes that are bitten short.) But other aspects of the kiss are not unfamiliar. For example, many Westerners like to pull each other's hair, rub noses, and even suck and bite their lover's lower lip. When I asked people whether they ever sucked their partner's lower lip, most said yes—which suggests that your lover may be amenable to trying some aspects of the Trobriand Islands kiss.

The Trobriand Islands kiss requires a wild and uninhibited nature. Practicing it may change you completely; but if you feel experimental, go ahead and set the ritual in motion. Let the savage in you free. Make tribal drums beat. And when your friends ask what happened to your eyelashes, simply smile and say, "Haven't you heard of the Trobriand Islands kiss?"

PART FOUR

Kissing Technique

$\mathcal{K}$ ISSING TECHNIQUE

A young college woman was dating a fellow who was a very good kisser. One night they were French kissing in her dorm when she suddenly sat back.

"I know this sounds crazy," she said, "but am I . . . well . . . am I *doing* it right?"

As she recalls, he proceeded to spend the next several hours showing her how to kiss better and enjoy it more, teaching her in particular how to be more aggressive with her tongue. Ah, if only all lessons and homework were like this! Without further delay, then, let's begin our course in contemporary kissing techniques.

To look or not to look

The question of whether lovers should kiss with their eyes open or closed is of fundamental importance. It was the question that prompted me to write this book, and I'm glad to be able to report some definitive answers here. More than two-thirds of those surveyed preferred to keep their eyes closed while kissing, but didn't mind if their partner kept his or hers open. Only one in three like to kiss with eyes open—and if *your* lover does, you can take it as a compliment. "I prefer kissing with my eyes open unless the girl isn't that pretty," said one twenty-four-year-old.

But you shouldn't worry about your appearance. If your partner kisses with his or her eyes open, everything will look out of focus. Indeed, because the brain interprets nearby faces as erotic, you'll actually appear sexier to your lover when you're mouth to mouth. So open your eyes, too, occasionally and enjoy the thrill!

"I like to see what my lover looks like and how he's responding."

"Sometimes the effect of prolonged eye contact is amazing."

"I like eyes open if I'm in love. I like to see my lover's eyes. It makes me feel connected soulfully to him."

"I usually kiss with my eyes closed because it's more romantic. But sometimes I like to peek at my husband, because his expression is so tender."

"I enjoy watching my boyfriend and me kiss. With my eyes open I'll turn my head to look in a mirror. It's quite a turn-on."

Talking while kissing

Silent lovers, listen to this! The majority of men and women (60 percent) enjoyed talking while kissing. "If my girlfriend won't talk to me while cuddling and kissing, I start to think she doesn't really like me," said one respondent. Why be bashful? After all, you're not kissing a stranger. Simply interrupt the kiss, and while still embracing your lover, say something nice. Then go back to the kiss. Next time you break lip contact, put your mouth right up to your lover's ear and whisper something erotic. Try some of the following phrases, which can be written discreetly on the palm of your hand.

- Oo!
- I love the way your _____(mouth, elbows, etc.) feel(s).
- Oogamanga, hubbamangah! (Gibberish can be sexy.)
- Oh, you little ****! (Four-letter word.)

Although most Westerners consider sex words taboo, about one in three couples use sexually charged or coarse language during kissing. One woman frankly admitted, "No, I have a problem with this and can't do it because of my Catholic upbringing." But those who talk dirty report that it's a turn-on to occasionally whisper something sexy to their partner between kisses. Sometimes such a comment will even get a laugh, which brings us to:

Laughing while kissing

If your partner laughs or giggles while kissing, don't get insulted. Sexual intimacy produces laughter in many people. Indeed, 80 percent of men and 96 percent of women reported that they sometimes giggled when kissing because of the pleasure they felt. And 2 percent even cried when a kiss felt too good to bear. So if your partner laughs while kissing, you know you're doing something *right*.

What to do with your hands while kissing

The initial contact between lovers is usually lip to lip; the hands may not even play a part in lovemaking until after the initial kisses. A man often likes a woman to cup his face in her hands while kissing him. It's a very tender and loving gesture. A woman may enjoy having a man run his fingers or hands up and down her spine. Here are some other suggestions:

WOMEN:
"I gently caress the back of his neck or his cheeks or run my fingers through his hair."

"I play with his hair, massage his muscles, pull his shirt out so I can feel the skin on his back."

"My hands are always moving—through his hair and over his back. Sometimes we clasp hands or a hand. My fingers touch his face (eyes, cheek, forehead, lips). My hands cup his ears. I also place my hands on his hips."

"If it's my husband, I'll touch his hair, his ears, his shoulders, back, buttocks, etc."

"I stroke the other person's head, arms, and body."

"I like to hold his face, rub his shoulders, rub his chest, and sometimes rub his leg."

"I explore his body, gently. Tease."

MEN:
"I usually rub her ass, upper leg, thigh, sides of breasts, ears, or even fingers."

"I usually put my hands around the girl's waist."

Kissing vs. being kissed

A subtle distinction! Many people wrote wonderful essays distinguishing *kissing* from *being kissed*, describing how they alternate between aggressive smooching one moment and passive receiving the next. Sometimes such unequal effort is simply delicious, like when you kiss someone who's docile, who merely tolerates the contact of your lips, who gives no clue whether they're burning up with desire or cool with antipathy until you finally sense, after perhaps minutes of anxiety, the slow throbbing response of their lips shuddering involuntarily and giving way to your dedicated assault so that your pulse skyrockets and your nerves tingle and sing.

"I can be kissed without kissing back and vice versa. It's possible to be passive and not actively involved with the kiss."

"It's a very fine line. You can be kissed by someone and they'll think you're kissing them back but in reality you're just there."

"I've told my boyfriend sometimes not to move while I kiss him. If he tries to respond while I'm kissing him, I tell him to be still—just to feel. This usually makes him very excited."

"You know what's really fun? When you kiss a guy and you tell him not to kiss you back, so that you're doing everything, guiding the entire kiss. It's such a sexy thing to do!"

Telephone kisses

Generally a favorite with kids, telephone kisses now and then find their way into the phone conversations of lovers. The technique simply involves making a kissing sound into your phone's receiver, usually before you hang up. Some people say they feel childish doing it, so you'll have to judge for yourself whether it's something you want to try.

MEN:
"My kids do it when they're saying good-bye on the phone to me. I do it, too. It's not so much silly or infantile, but sort of . . . childlike."

"Just a smooch now and then. Most of the time, verbal romance via the phone makes me feel awkward."

"No. It sounds stupid and makes the receiver all juicy."

WOMEN:
"I've kissed over the phone as a goofy joke. I think it's a fun/silly thing to do. I pucker up and suck air through my lips and make a *looonnng* kissing sound. It can be a bit rude, but it's funny."

"I love nice juicy phone kisses. I have a phone friend who I met on the phone from a wrong number. He calls and kisses me without even saying hello. I love it."

"I do it all the time."

"I do it, but I don't like the sound over the phone."

"Yes, I explain to whomever exactly how I am going to kiss them when I get them alone."

"My daughter and I have developed our own kiss to each other. It starts off with an *mmm* sound which is extended into a smack by saying *mmm-uuuu*—it's a verbal kiss."

"I see my boyfriend only on weekends (he lives fifty miles

away), and we talk on the phone every night, so we'll often end our conversations with a kiss over the phone.''

"Yes. I say, 'Close your eyes. Think of me, take a very deep breath, and let's kiss!' ''

When to kiss on a date

Lovers Frank and Sally haven't seen each other for three days. They're going out tonight to a movie. As Frank walks up to her door he's thinking, "I can't wait to see her." He doesn't even know it himself, but a keenly pleasurable anticipation is making his palms sweat. His breath comes quick as he rings the bell, and in the back of his mind he has a warm and comfortable expectation of how wonderful and right the world becomes whenever he's with Sally.

Inside, Sally is tying her hair with a ribbon when the doorbell rings. "It's him!" she says to herself, her heart racing, her throat tight and dry. Frank walks into the living room, and they gaze at each other for a full minute, both feeling an intense happiness mixed with an acute longing for each other. They're standing only three or four feet apart when an invisible force seems to drive them together, and they begin to move in for a quick hello kiss. Sally's eyes smile more and more the nearer she gets to Frank. Frank can't wait to be near her and can't believe his luck in getting a kiss so early in the date! As they get closer both maintain eye contact, almost up to the last fraction of a second before their lips meet. They kiss each other briefly but passionately on the lips, a kiss that communicates what they're feeling much better than words can, something which if you were forced to put it into writing would read, "We're perfect for each other!"

Some people enjoy a quick kiss at the beginning of a date, when they first meet. These greeting kisses seem to work best with a couple like Frank and Sally who know each other fairly well. Others seem to think there is an unwritten formal code of dating that *obliges* a couple to kiss at the outset of a date. While there really isn't any formal code requiring a kiss at the outset, it can be an easy way to break the ice.

"In the beginning we kiss on the side of the face to say hello."

"You should kiss at the outset as a friendly gesture of saying hello."

"At the beginning of the date a formal kiss can be expected."

"People should kiss when they feel most comfortable kissing each other. For some people it's when they first meet."

But one young woman expressed a diametrically contrary opinion:

"You definitely should not kiss when you meet your date."

And this brings us to the perennial question of whether you should kiss on a *first* date. When Sally met Frank she told him that she didn't kiss boys until the *sixth* date. Knowing this, Frank quickly invited her out six nights in a row so that he could get through the first five nonkissing dates to the sixth date, at which time Sally allowed a first kiss. While you may not have such hard-and-fast rules, many young people seem to think that you shouldn't kiss on a first date. At the same time, an almost equal number think it's perfectly all right—

The Nays:
"No kissing during the date if it's the first date. But if you've been going out, that's different, and kissing can go on during the date if wanted."

"If it's your first date you probably shouldn't kiss."

"If it's the first date—unless it's an exceptionally good date—you shouldn't kiss."

"The question of when to kiss on a date varies depending on the person you're dating. Most of the time I don't kiss on a first date, but that's because I don't have any intentions of seeing this person again."

The Yeas:
"On the first few dates you can kiss near the end of the date when saying good night."

"On a first date I think you should kiss when you say good night. After you've dated someone for a while you should kiss when you meet your date *and* when saying good night."

"Depends on how long you've been dating. I dated a guy for eight months and we kissed all the time toward the end of the relationship. At first, I think it's best to pop a kiss at the onset of a date, then have a nice kiss good night."

"It depends on your relationship with the person. If you're going on your first date, probably you should kiss at the end. But if you know him and have been seeing him for a while, you should kiss anytime you want to. I'm sure the other person is always willing."

The thing to remember is that the kiss will come much more easily if you're on the same wavelength as your date before you attempt it. Keep the conversation going, gaze into each other's eyes for long periods of time, and let the excitement mount between you. Someone once said that if you look into anyone's eyes for five minutes you'll fall in love with them. Plenty of eye contact will get you in tune with each other so that the kiss seems like the natural thing to do.

Here are some tips for when to kiss on a date:

- When you leave a restaurant and you're standing close together trying to decide where to go.
- When at a museum together and you're close and examining a work of art.
- In the middle of the date after you've had a good conversation and have made eye contact for an extended time.
- After you make some funny joke and you're both laughing together and in a good mood.

When during the course of a date should one kiss?
WOMEN:
"Whenever lips are remotely *near each other*, and definitely at the end of the date."

"Usually after a good two hours, or once the two people are comfortable together. For me, this usually takes place after a long talk or dinner. After the date—definitely, it's kind of a courtesy, a thank-you of sorts. During the date if the situation (mood) dictates."

"I think that at any time during the date it's appropriate to kiss. If the moment's right, do it."

"You should kiss at the least expected time during a date, in order to make the date more fun and exciting."

"Halfway through the date. You should know by then if you like what you see. So you have to test the waters."

MEN:
"I like to kiss at the end of a date."

"It definitely depends on where the date is. For example, if you take your date to the movies you might want to find a seat in the back corner of the theater and as soon as the lights dim you can make your move. I've had kisses that lasted the length of the film. If you don't know your date too well this might not be the best time to do it because you might find a fist down your throat instead of a tongue."

"I always let the girl do what she wants when she wants to."

The make-up kiss

One of the most delightful thrills of being in love is getting over a quarrel and making up. Throughout the ages lovers have argued over the silliest things, getting angry and vowing never to see each other again. Then inevitably—sometimes within a matter of minutes or even seconds—they become reconciled, and all their angry emotions are transmuted into the most enraptured devotion; they feel they've never been closer. With your differences ironed out, you'll enjoy a new lease on love. The kiss (known as *Versöhnungskuss* in German) that marks such a turning point celebrates a special and wonderful experiment in the alchemy of the heart. Work your own magic like this:

- If you're still mad at each other, approach carefully, giving no sign of what you intend. Let your partner think you simply want to make another comment.
- Just before you kiss, quickly say something conciliatory, for example, "Let's make love, not war."
- Deliver a little kiss to test the waters.
- If your initial peck is accepted, follow it up *immediately* with a more prolonged kiss.
- If you've just argued, you'll both feel the heat of anger transformed into the ecstasy of reconciliation.

The French, who are always attuned to matters of the heart, had a tradition in the theater during Molière's time that involved love scenes of reconciliation. Such scenes often appeared in comedies, which suggests an important point about the make-up kiss: Keep your sense of humor about you as you do the kiss. Attempt it boldly during the heat of an argument when an incongruous gesture of reconciliation may bring first a smile and then a laugh of pleasure to your lover's lips.

How to kiss at the movies

Surprisingly, most people said they didn't like to kiss at the movies; they prefer watching the film. The 30 percent of men and 40 percent of women who do like to kiss in a theater don't like to have people sitting behind them when they kiss. And they usually kiss during romantic or tender moments or when the lights first go down. Kisses in a theater aren't too passionate; they're more likely to be short pecks.

If your partner enjoys kissing at the movies, teach him or her the copy-cat game: You kiss whenever the actors do. Of course this works best at romantic films.

WOMEN:
"Generally I don't like doing it when there are people behind me. I've kissed when there are heartwarming scenes, for example, families coming together or beautiful scenes of nature. It's close and warm being next to my boyfriend in a dark and nonintimate setting."

"I don't like to kiss, but I do *love* to grope at the movies, almost to the point of excruciation!"

"Kissing at the movies is okay, but I won't do it if people are behind us; I think that's rude."

"I do it sometimes when the movie's bad."

"Maybe one or two small kisses in a movie. During a romantic or emotional part that we both can relate to."

"If a movie doesn't hold my attention, I feel I might as well enjoy something."

"I kiss during romantic scenes, and hold hands tightly during scary scenes."

"I usually kiss during sappy parts."

How to kiss in a car

So many survey respondents (98 percent) said they enjoyed kissing in cars that it's a wonder car manufacturers don't list "plenty of room for kissing" as a feature in their advertising pitch. Here are just a few comments on when, where, and how to do it.

"I sometimes kiss my husband on the lips while he's driving. This technique requires careful consideration in angling my head so as not to block the driver's view. Kissing in cars is awkward—you have to reach and twist and it usually lacks the meaningful physical connection."

"We kiss at traffic lights."

"My boyfriend usually drives, and when the car is moving I generally give him cheek kisses due to the angle. When the car stops at a light he'll turn his face to me and we'll kiss on the lips. Sometimes we've even kissed on the lips while the car is moving, but we do that only when traffic is light."

"Always good-bye and hello pecks, when people drop me off or pick me up."

"When I kiss with a date in a car, it usually takes place in the front seat. It is always fun to watch the windows eventually fog up, too! It's exciting."

"I kiss in a parked car as foreplay."

"When I was on vacation in the Caribbean with my current lover, we drove to a beautiful mountaintop with a great view and kissed. I felt like a teenager parking at a drive-in or Lover's Leap."

"It's exciting to kiss in a car because it's more awkward to go all the way. I guess I like kissing in awkward places, cars being one example *only*."

"Of course I kiss in the car. That's where we all learned. Back seats even!"

"What *didn't* I do in a car? I like to surprise my husband with a kiss on his ear or neck while he's driving. Also I've made out at drive-ins (about ten years ago when I was sixteen)."

"If we're in the car and they play romantic music, we kiss no matter where we are."

"I love parking and kissing, though it's difficult to find a place that's private and safe."

"Car kisses are very exciting. The chance that someone will see us kissing adds to the excitement."

"Even though I'm a full-grown adult, there's a certain thrill in this—especially parked on a public street. I think I'm a bit of an exhibitionist!"

How to kiss at parties

Imagine a boy and girl at a party: They're talking to each other when suddenly they notice they're alone in a corner and no one's looking. The excitement has been building between them all evening, and now the moment is right. Quickly they kiss, a stolen kiss, and suddenly a flame ignites in both their hearts, so that even when they wander apart later and talk to other people during the party, they're linked because of that kiss. Such an experience is quite common; in fact, about 80 percent of people like to kiss at parties. Usually they do it off to the side so as not to make a scene.

WOMEN:
"Sometimes outside or in another room or in the bathroom

or just in a corner. I wish I had a chance to do this again soon!''

"When I kiss at parties I usually give kisses on the cheek or quick pecks on the lips. But if I'm dancing and am physically close to my boyfriend and the music and/or the moment is romantic, I'll deliver a long-lasting kiss and for a brief moment will sometimes French kiss.''

"I just take his face and turn it toward me and kiss, kiss, kiss.''

"At parties I kiss in the bathroom, in a closet, on the dance floor, in a crowded room, in a quiet corner. There are lots of options.''

"I kiss at parties behind kitchen doors, in halls, on the back porch, in the basement, or on the staircase if it's dark.''

"I usually kiss my friends hello at parties, and often good-bye. I usually kiss them on the cheek, and give them a hug, too.''

"While dancing I kiss an ear.''

"Stolen candies—and kisses—are the sweetest.''

"I like to kiss the men at the party good night with a quick peck on the lips.''

"You can sometimes pretend to whisper and give a small kiss in your lover's ear—this can be discreet and exciting.''

Kissing games

You're never too old for kissing games, and here are some classics that will please lovers of any age:

- *Copy-cat.* In a movie theater or while watching TV, you kiss whenever the actors do.
- *Truth or Dare.* One person at a time is asked embarrassing questions, and if the group votes that he's lying, he has to take a dare, such as giving one of the girls a French kiss.
- *Freeze Tag.* A group of friends runs around the house, and one person is selected to be the freezer, running after the others, attempting to kiss them. When the freezer kisses you, you remain frozen until anyone else unfreezes you with a kiss.
- *Spin the Bottle.* One person spins a bottle. If it points to a person of the opposite sex, they kiss in front of the group. In a dark room the game is played with a flashlight instead of a bottle.
- *Post Office.* All the girls are out of the room, and an area is partitioned off as a post office, with one boy inside it. One of the other boys tells one of the girls she has some mail. She goes into the post office and is kissed. She exits and the game continues with girls being called in one by one.
- *The Candy Kissing Game.* Have your lover go into another room and eat or drink something sweet and then immediately come back into the room and kiss you. You have to guess what your partner just ate or drank. This little guessing game is a delicious way to spend an afternoon. The diversion of having one of the lovers periodically leave the room will tantalize the other to the point of fainting excitement.
- *The Guessing Game.* While kissing, mention a number of foreign or slang terms (like smooching or sparking) and ask your partner which one he or she thinks best describes what you're doing. (See the list on pages 137–138.) For

example, "Are we spooning or smacking?" Then kiss your partner and let him or her guess.

- *The Train Game.* While traveling together on a train or in a car, whoever spots a barn (or a red car, or anything else you select) can kiss the other.
- *Kissing by the Book.* Enlist your lover as a study partner and work your way through this book, using it as a text. Schedule plenty of quizzes, seminars, and a final exam.

Want instructions for over forty more kissing games? See *Kissing Games: A Study in Folklore*, by Susan McDonald and David J. Gerrick (Loraine, Ohio: Dayton Labs, 1982).

Social and business greeting kisses

You've known about social greeting kisses all your life, since they're the type of kiss you give and receive when you're at family gatherings. But not many people realize that the same greeting kiss is becoming increasingly appropriate in some business settings. In fact the larger the city, the more likely business people are to kiss in greeting one another. The custom also tends to be industry specific: people in certain fields—entertainers, consultants, human resources workers, and some health care employees—are more likely to kiss than people in manufacturing, medicine, banking, and accounting. Here are the basic dos and don'ts for the business kiss:

Do:
- Kiss in a business situation only if you feel comfortable doing it and know the person well.

- Kiss at business parties and other social functions, like the annual baseball game, award ceremonies, picnics, or conventions.
- Merely touch cheeks and kiss the air. You could also kiss the person's cheek if you're not wearing lipstick.
- Let your boss initiate the kiss.

DON'T:
- Don't kiss strangers. A kiss on first meeting someone is usually inappropriate.
- Don't kiss in strictly business environments like offices, courts, banks, restaurant meetings, and auditoriums.
- Don't let people kiss you if you feel uncomfortable about it. To avoid a kiss simply stand at arm's length and thrust your hand forward for a handshake.
- Don't kiss directly on the lips.
- Don't smudge your business associate with lipstick; if you're wearing lipstick, simply touch cheeks.
- Don't kiss drunk business associates; they may misinterpret the kiss as a sexual advance.

How to avoid kissing diseases

We'll define a kissing disease as one you can get simply by kissing someone. While this includes infections like the flu, mononucleosis, and more severe things like syphilis and herpes, the good news is that AIDS is not a kissing disease: There are no known cases of AIDS being transmitted by kissing. Levels of the HIV virus in an infected person's saliva are so low that physicians believe there is very little danger of getting AIDS by kissing. If both parties were kissing with bleeding cuts in their mouths through which the HIV virus could pass directly from bloodstream to bloodstream, that would be a different story. In short, it's highly unlikely that you'll get AIDS from kissing your boyfriend or girlfriend.

You could, however, get mononucleosis from kissing your lover. Mononucleosis, also known as the kissing disease, has become something of a badge of honor for teenagers. With pride they boast to friends and teachers that they can't go to school because they have "mono." The disease is transmitted by kissing (hence the nickname) or by other close personal contact, and it's most common where young people aged between fifteen and twenty-five live together. In colleges and universities the estimated incidence may be as high as 300 to 1,500 cases per 100,000 students. Most people become immune to mono by the time they're forty because they're exposed to a mild form of the disease and develop antibodies. But since there's no way to prevent mono, the best you can do is avoid kissing someone who has it or who's recovering from it.

With other diseases that can be transmitted through kissing—including flu viruses, herpes, syphilis, etc.—the answer is unfortunately just as vague. One of the chief epidemiologists in the Northeast has said that the best advice the medical profession can give people today about avoiding kissing diseases is simply to use common sense—if you *do* know people who are sick with a communicable disease (for example, if you can see sores on their lips, or you hear them coughing excessively), don't kiss them. There isn't much more you can do. Without a lab test, it's often impossible to know if someone has a communicable disease—the infected person often doesn't know it either. It seems that the medical profession is as advanced on this one as they are on the common cold.

How to add tenderness to your kisses

One young woman complained that many of the boys she kissed seemed to have stiff wooden mouths. "They need to practice movement in their lips," she said. "I don't know how else to describe it." Another woman said, "I feel like telling guys, 'Soften those lips or you get no kiss.' You can tell a person's mood by how soft their lips are." Some other women complained that men weren't tender enough when kissing. In general, women seemed to understand better than men how to be sensitive and responsive during mouth-to-mouth contact. The technique really stems from having empathy; as one young woman put it, you've got to *listen* to how your lover kisses you. Try the following to become more receptive and sensitive in your kissing:

- Force yourself to become passive so that you stop leading the kiss.
- Take a deep breath and relax.
- Let your partner initiate new kissing techniques.
- Move your lips slowly during the kiss itself.
- Sway your head gently from side to side.
- Try to imagine how your partner is feeling.
- Eat apples. (This will expend some of your oral aggression so that you'll be content with soft kisses.)
- Practice gentle lip and tongue movement on hard candy and then use the same movements during kissing.

How to talk about kissing

"Everyone should express their kissing needs to their partners, since it can be a fulfilling and bonding experience," said a twenty-seven-year-old woman in response to a survey question.

Another young woman said that the most difficult thing in the world for her was to tell some guy how to kiss differently. She wanted to give her boyfriend pointers so he would kiss better, but she never did it because she simply didn't know how to tell him.

Unfortunately, we live in a society that generally discourages talking about sexual matters. Other cultures, such as natives of certain South Sea islands, including the Trobriands, are much more comfortable talking about things like kissing. Studies show, however, that both men and women like people who occasionally talk about sex. And after you read this book, you'll have plenty to talk about! Talking about kissing can be a fun and sexy thing to do. And you'll be surprised at how quickly *talking* about kissing can lead to doing it. Here are some suggestions for how and when to talk about kissing:

- After a movie discuss how the actors kissed. Guys should generally praise how the women actors kissed. This will subtly flatter your girlfriend.
- Want to seem like a worldly and knowledgeable lover? If you see people kissing in public, comment to your lover on their technique.
- When you're on a date and you feel the attraction building between you, start talking about kissing at every opportunity.
- Ask your partner questions about kissing. It doesn't matter if you already know the answers—ask anyway. This will convince your date that you value his or her opinion.

- After a kiss discuss one or more aspects of it with your partner. You might begin by saying something positive about their kissing ability, something that will make them feel good. If you can't think of anything to say, try one of these phrases:
    —I love the way you kiss.
    —You have a nice lower lip.
    —Kiss me like that again!
    —Where did you learn to kiss so deliciously!
    —That's the sexiest kiss I ever got.
- Bring this book with you on dates and ask your partner to select one or two kisses from the kissing encyclopedia that you can try together.

Probably the most important reason to talk about kissing is that even though you're compatible in every other way, you and your partner may have different views about how to kiss. One young woman said, "My boyfriend doesn't like ear kisses; he says they tickle too much. As a result, he doesn't think I'll like them either, which is dead wrong. They really turn me on!" Her complaint is a common one—many lovers have kissing preferences that their partner doesn't know about. When I asked whether people had different views about kissing from their partner, about 65 percent said yes. Many women reported that they liked to kiss more than their lover. Said one twenty-six-year-old: "I definitely like to kiss more than my husband does. I wish he got into it more." So, remember, *always ask what your partner likes*—it may be totally different from what you think.

♥ ♥ ♥

"We've read enough!" I can hear some readers clamoring. "We're ready to close the book and kiss!"

And indeed you are, since you've been prepared by hundreds of people who have told you what they like about kissing, how they do it, and what it means to them. You know more about the subject than an army of lovers. You're ready to kiss! Find your boyfriend, girlfriend, sweetheart, your soul mate, your honey, your sugar pie, your darling and pucker up! And when your lover gasps in delight and breaks off from a passionate embrace demanding that you admit where you learned to kiss like the gods of love themselves, merely contain your chuckle of triumph, smile to yourself, candidly point to your copy of this book, and prepare to revel in the sensual pleasures that belong to all who have mastered the art of kissing.

A CHANCE FOR READERS TO RESPOND

Do you have any kissing experiences you'd like to share? Are there other types of kisses you'd like to describe? If so, I'd like to hear from you. Remember that all responses will remain anonymous, and by sending your comments, you agree that they may be used, anonymously, in future editions of *The Art of Kissing*.

If you would like to participate in my next project—a study of dating practices and attitudes—please drop me a business-size, self-addressed, stamped envelope and I'll send you a questionnaire to fill out. All responses will be anonymous. *Thank you!*

Please send your comments and correspondence to:

William Cane
P.O. Box 1422
Brookline, MA 02146-0011